Embrace the Journey

Becky Murray's Story

BECKY MURRAY & RALPH TURNER

Sarah GRACE PUBLISHING
Dyslexic Friendly

First published 2020 by Sarah Grace Publishing
an imprint of Malcolm Down Publishing Ltd
www.malcolmdown.co.uk

24 23 22 21 20   7 6 5 4 3 2 1

British Library Cataloguing in Publication Data
A catalogue record for this book is available from the British Library.

ISBN 978-1-912863-54-9

Cover design by Esther Kotecha
Art direction by Sarah Grace
Printed in the UK

Some names have been changed to protect identities.

Commendations

Becky Murray's book *Embrace the Journey* will challenge you to strive to do great things for Christ. Now more than ever do we need evangelists and missionaries to say yes to Jesus and run with the call of God. Becky is doing that and I believe you will be encouraged by her faith, stories and testimony. Get ready to embrace your journey!

Dr R.T. Kendall
Author, Former Senior Minister, Westminster Chapel

Every reader will be deeply challenged by this book for a number of reasons, not least of all because you will discover through Becky's story the genius of God to take the apparent ordinary and make it extraordinary. Of course it was only possible because Becky Murray just kept saying 'YES'. Yes to the challenge, yes to the sacrifice, yes through the trials and yes to loving unconditionally those who need more than anything simply to feel loved.

As in the words of Heidi Bakker 'Love looks like something', and Matt and Becky have demonstrated in a tangible way what the 'Love of God' looks like to hundreds of children around the world.

Ken Gott
Founder and Leader, House of Prayer Europe

I have known Becky Murray since 2002. During that time I have witnessed the call of God and the passion He has placed in her heart, to reach humanity with the love of Christ. The mandate to reach the 'one' has birthed a ministry that is reaching thousands of lives, including the orphan and the widow, with the gospel of Jesus Christ. This book will reveal what God will do when we surrender to the Holy Spirit and allow Him to use us as the hands and feet of Jesus. Through the life of Becky and her husband Matthew, you will be encouraged that, even through the darkest of times, God has always shown Himself mighty to save! I know this book will ignite your heart to follow your call and embrace the journey.

Nathan Morris
Founder and President, Shake the Nations

As you read this book you will quickly discover there is more to it than what we so easily call destiny. You will feel the providence of God in each word and story. I know personally that Becky's life was changed by a preposition, by the word 'INTO'. . . she dared to go (into) the world and today children by the thousands are benefitting from her obedience.

People of providence have a window of opportunity that they must step through and this is exactly what has taken place in Becky Murray's life. She has, as I would say, crawled into the eyes of Jesus and seen the abandoned, the broken and the defenceless as He would see them. An anonymous poet wrote her story long ago.

> Love has a hem in its garment
> That reaches the very dust.
> It reaches each stain in the street and the lane,
> And because it can it must.

She is an answer to prayer for many and her boldness takes her into places others would never dare to go. Her life is a challenge to those who feel the call to mission on their life. Those she is used to rescue and bless can gratefully say, 'Thank you, Becky, for saying yes.'

Cleddie Keith
Senior Pastor, Heritage Fellowship, Florence, Kentucky, USA

I have known Becky for many years and in that time it has been a joy to see the woman God created collide with the purpose He designed her for. Becky is a woman uncompromising in faith, generous in heart and relentless in commitment. She has a deep love for Jesus, a passion for His church and an infectious zeal for a lost world. Whether you read this book or meet her in person, you will encounter a Jesus-follower who embodies the single-minded devotion to the Lord and His cause. You will be challenged, convicted, provoked, encouraged and hopefully inspired by her life and what you read. Jump in, embrace her story and maybe you too will end up embracing His journey!

Dr John Andrews

This compelling book is the account of what happens when a woman intentionally seeks to share the love of Christ with those who have little or no material resources of their own. Challenged when just a small child to fulfil a vision for missionary work, Becky Murray fulfils her dream as she and her husband Matthew launch the OneByOne ministry. I have known Becky for several years and have been amazed at her tireless commitment to serve others and her tenacious resolve to act in obedience to the call of God on her life. I unreservedly commend both her and her ministry. You will be inspired and challenged by what you are about to read.

John Glass
General Superintendent, Elim Pentecostal Churches 2000–2016
Chair of Council Evangelical Alliance 2014–2018

Becky is a woman after God's own heart. You can see this through her work with OneByOne and the King's Children's Home. Her passion and gift to provide the children with a safe haven and education shines in our studios and through to our viewers' screens. It's always a pleasure to work with her as she delivers meaningful content, and we are looking forward to embracing more seasons with her.

Emily Martin
Production Manager, TBN UK

Wow!! Faith-creating and hope-giving, *Embrace the Journey* is filled with supernatural stories intersecting with the lives of ordinary people. It's not just Becky's story but a rich tapestry of God's hand at work in the lives of many. You will be inspired to believe God for the same supernatural interactions as you embrace your God journey.

Steve Uppal
Senior Leader, All Nations Church, Wolverhampton UK

Acknowledgements

Thank yous from Becky

Thank you to Ralph for capturing my stories so beautifully and thoroughly.

Thank you to all our amazing team at OneByOne, whether you're based in the UK, USA, Kenya or Pakistan. One of my greatest honours is working alongside people who are filled with passion and compassion. You guys inspire me every day.

Finally, and most importantly, thank you to my husband Matthew and son Josiah. You two bring so much love and joy to my life. Thank you for your patience with me when I'm often out of the country and for standing side by side with me in this adventure of serving Jesus together. I love you both very much.

Thank yous from Ralph

Thank you to Becky and Matt for allowing me to help tell their story. It is a privilege to share in, albeit via the written page, the incredible work they are doing around the world.

Thank you as always to my wife Roh for her constant encouragement to keep writing, and for her help with interviewing Becky.

A big thank you to my regular proofreaders, Ali Pereria and John Flavell, and to Alison Leigh who has joined the team. Thank you to Malcolm Down and his colleagues – professional and supportive as always.

Contents

Foreword

Becky Murray is what I'd call modern old-school – she sees the need and answers the call with no hesitation. She's a woman who isn't afraid to pay the price of full-time ministry and all that it requires. I'm proud to call her and Matthew my friends.

Over the last few years I've witnessed Matthew and Becky's endurance and commitment to the ministry that God has given them. It's been fascinating to see how OneByOne has grown into such an incredible organisation that is reaching thousands of lives.

OneByOne is a ministry that is fulfilling its name: focusing on the one, reaching the one, doing as much as possible for the one. God has blessed them with open doors and open hearts to reach one by one. I believe in what they're doing and I look forward to the ways God is going to lead Matthew and Becky as they continue to press forward.

For years I've talked about the need being the call; it doesn't take a compelling word with angelic interpretation. All it takes is seeing the need and responding to that call. Becky Murray is an example of this. She sees needs and responds. Whether it's street children in Pakistan, orphans in Kenya or girls at risk of human trafficking across the world, she is there, when these kids need someone the most; someone who is an extension of Christ at work.

When I found out Becky was writing a book I wasn't surprised. Her story needs to be told and it needs to be shared. I know these pages will bless you as her stories always bless me. I've spent time with Becky in the UK, in New York City at our Metro World Child headquarters where she has spoken to our staff and interns, and I've visited their home in Kenya too. I've been to some places in my time, but few are as remote as Bumala B, the little village in western Kenya where God has chosen to pour out His Spirit through OneByOne.

As you know, I've never shied away from dangerous and tough environments, so without hesitation we decided to partner with Matthew and Becky and today we are reaching more than 10,000 children in this setting. That's the power of partnership and that's why I love these guys. They just get it.

More than ever we need people like Becky Murray who fearlessly say yes to the call of God. I pray that as you digest the stories and the lessons in these pages, you too will embrace the journey that God has planned for you.

Bill Wilson
Founder, Metro World Child

Introduction

She stood in the market square, holding his hand and helping to translate.

Tall for her age, though desperately thin, Felicity was nine. She'd noticed me talking to six-year-old Solomon, another street kid in the city of Bo, Sierra Leone. And she'd come over to help.

I didn't know it just then, but my life was about to change.

Solomon spoke no English but, with Felicity's help, I got to understand how both of them were on the streets. They were begging. They were well known in this dusty square, with its wooden bench stalls and its piles of second-hand clothes for sale. Solomon was begging on behalf of his grandparents, because he could get more money than they could. Felicity seemed to be on her own, and never mentioned any family.

My friend Amanda and I helped them both. We bought some second-hand clothes from a market stall to replace the rags that Solomon was wearing. And for Felicity I bought some pink flip-flops.

I'd noticed straight away that Felicity was barefooted, and it seemed a small gesture to get her the flip-flops. She chose the pink ones and it cost me all of about fifty pence in UK money.

I invited the two of them to join us later that day when we were to drive out to an open-air meeting.

As I stepped out of the hotel in the early evening, the sun was going down and the dust from the streets was beginning to settle as the traffic lessened. I saw two children running towards me. Felicity and Solomon. They sprinted over and gave me the biggest of hugs. I was delighted they had remembered, and pointed them to the vehicle we were travelling in.

'But don't you want me to go to your room?' Felicity asked.

I didn't understand.

'No. We're going right now. There's room in the vehicle – in you get!'

'Shouldn't I wait in your hotel room?' Felicity repeated.

It was then that it hit me. I was a woman in her twenties at the time, and the little girl for whom I'd bought fifty-pence pink flip-flops thought that I was doing it for sexual favours.

My mind was racing. How could she think that? What terrible things had happened in her nine-year-old life for her to even go there in her mind?

I looked at her. And I was angry.

Angry with all the poverty and corruption. Angry with the abusive men and women who could do that to a child. Angry that Felicity had been robbed of her childhood.

And that's when I knew. The promises God had given me years before regarding working with children in poverty were no longer just promises. It was time.

Felicity's face became my personal non-negotiable moment with God. He had called me. Standing in front of me was very the reason for the call.

I knew what I had to do.

Chapter One
The Bar of Chocolate

'Mummy, when I grw up I'm going to be a missionary to Africa.'

Mum tells me that I was about four at the time I declared this. There's no real background to it, other than we went to church and I must have picked up something about missionaries from a conversation there, or from one of my first Sunday school sessions.

But there it was. Not even five and I was talking about Africa.

The Bible says we are fearfully and wonderfully made. In fact, Psalm 139 says that 'my soul knows it very well'. There's more going on there than just being made physically. It's our *soul* that knows it very well – our inner being, not just our outer body. I believe God plans our paths from the beginning of time and that includes our calling.

So there I was, aged four and God's call was already being worked out.

That early passion for Africa found its way into my childhood in a number of ways. I paid particular attention when missionaries were visiting our church. Mum says I was glued to the television screen the first time I saw a black newsreader on the BBC (Moira Stuart, I think). And then there was the chocolate bar.

Blue Riband

A Blue Riband chocolate bar to be exact. A special treat for me and my two sisters. Donna is eight years older than me, and Wendy six years older, so I'm the baby of the family.

As we sat in front of the TV screen, the programme we were watching on ITV switched to a commercial break. It was not uncommon for television channels to promote charitable causes and before the advert for something like Daz or Omo washing detergent, on came a donation request for the famine in Ethiopia.

I was caught by it. At four years old, my heart went out to the malnourished girl I saw on the screen. She was a similar age but so obviously desperately hungry; a look of pain across her face.

'Eat your chocolate bar, Darling.'

I had started the Blue Riband but now it was simply held, slowly melting with the heat of my hand, as I remained transfixed by the screen.

'No, Mummy. Send it to them!'

It took quite a bit of persuasion from my mum to get me to eat the rest of it. She explained that they would not want my chocolate bar.

But how about my life? They may not want a chocolate bar . . . but would they want me? Even at four years old, God was working out my future path.

Happy Families

Do you remember the card game 'Happy Families'? Lots of fun for kids of course. And it reflects well the family I was part of. It really was a happy family.

Home was Rhodes Avenue, Kimberworth Park, Rotherham. I lived in our council house there, right up until I left home to be married.

It was a joyful place, full of laughter. Mum made sure of that. She was a cleaner by profession, and a great mum. The house itself was just a post-war council house, but it was such a loving home and family.

Dad was a carer when I was young, moving on to be a postman later in life. He was also passionate about Jesus. A lay preacher and deacon in our local church, he was keen that his whole family were with him on a Sunday. That church was called Station Road Masbrough Assemblies of God, later to change its name to Liberty Church, Rotherham.

That's where you would find me on a Sunday, from an early age, holding on to Mum's hand as we walked through the doors. I was excited to go. I loved church – the people, the worship, and the Sunday school lessons.

Actually, you would find me in quite a few different churches growing up. As a lay preacher, Dad was invited to speak all over the Rotherham area and sometimes further afield. I still drive past various church buildings with memories of Dad speaking there.

Church was an almost daily event as well. Most evenings we would either be at evening meetings, or home with visitors that Mum and Dad would be counselling.

Almost a daily event . . . but not quite. Saturday night was family night. The house phone would be unplugged, the door locked and the five of us would gather in the lounge. Sometimes we'd play board games, but most of the time we'd watch whatever was on TV. I have vivid memories of *The A Team*, *Gladiators* and *Blind Date*!

Christmas

Dad was like a grown-up kid on occasions, more excited about birthdays and Christmas than we were. I have this abiding memory of Dad with his big camcorder – probably the most expensive piece of kit he ever owned – running around the house at Christmas, poking the camera in our faces, shouting out that Christmas had come!

Like any young child, I loved Christmas. Wendy, older than me by six years, rather spoiled it for me.

I was about seven years old when Wendy came into my bedroom on Christmas Eve. In a sing-song voice she chanted, 'I know something you don't know!'

Of course the something related to Father Christmas. I think I've just about forgiven her.

Aside from the stockings in the room for Father Christmas to fill (sweets, an apple and a shiny new one-penny piece) there were always piles of presents around the Christmas tree in the lounge, and even an order in which we were allowed to enter the room in the morning. Dad first, then Mum, then the three daughters in age order. So I was always last. Not that it really mattered. The thrill of seeing the tree with the lights on, fully decorated and, more to the point, the enormous pile of presents around it, made up for any delay in getting into the room.

Like our treasured Saturdays, Christmas was a family day too. It was the one time we didn't go to the church meeting. As a family, after the present opening, we'd get dressed up in smart clothes and Mum and Dad would prepare for Christmas lunch while I played with my new toys. The Queen's speech was insisted upon, often followed by one of two films we had on VHS: *Chitty Chitty Bang Bang* or *The Sound of Music*.

Dad was such a family man, no more so than at Christmas. And such a joker. When we were very little, Dad would insist that the three of us sisters stood all the way through the Queen's speech. It wasn't him being a royalist, it was him being naughty!

Actually, there were going to be four children. That's what Mum and Dad had planned. Two older, then two younger. The idea was to have another child after me but I was such a terrible baby, Mum and Dad decided that was enough!

Looking back, I think it was probably colic or something like that which kept me crying for seemingly days on end. But it wasn't diagnosed at the time, so I cried. And cried. Poor Mum and Dad. They certainly knew I was around.

The Mask

Emma and Danielle were my best friends at Roughwood Primary School. We'd have a lot of fun, didn't always pay attention in the lessons and would joke about a lot. I liked to be popular and, even at nine years old, I was aware that I was presenting myself in one way at school and as somebody different at home and church.

On Sundays, my church friend Hannah Russell and I would usually sit together and, whilst the talk was going on, would quietly draw or whisper to each other. Sometimes we'd even sneak out to play 'hide and seek'. But that Sunday in September 1990 was different. The youth group were taking the service that evening, which was unusual. And instead of the 'preach', many of them were telling their own stories.

I can't really remember what they said, but one of the stories must have been about someone wearing a mask – pretending to be one type of person and not really being themselves.

As a nine-year-old girl, these words struck home. I knew I was acting differently at school. And even at nine, I wanted to love and follow God wholeheartedly. My parents' faith was so vivid. I had caught their passion, though maybe not fully understood what was meant by a Christian faith.

At the end of the youth presentation, there was an invitation for anyone to come to the front of the meeting who wanted to know Jesus as their personal saviour. I didn't need a second invitation.

Walking quickly to the front, I was led into the pastor's study at the back, and there prayed a prayer:

'Lord Jesus, please forgive me for living without You. Please forgive me for wearing a mask and not being the person You want me to be. Please come into my life. I invite You into my heart. Amen.'

As I came back into the meeting room, there were Mum and Dad. Both of them crying. So many hugs.

My grandad, who was an elder in the church, gave me a Bible to commemorate the occasion. The date had been written on the top and Grandad had inscribed:

To our dearest Becky on this day, the day your life changed. We are so proud of the step you have taken today. With love, Grandad and Grandma.

Slow Journey

To be honest, I was slow to realise how much God loved me. From that first prayer, it was a gentle faith journey. Some people come to salvation and immediately have a revelation of how much God loves them but, for me, this took a little while longer to sink in.

I remember days in my bedroom growing up, pondering on God's love. As I grew into my teens, I began to wonder about how much He loved me. I maybe even doubted it on occasion – despite having such a loving and supportive family and church.

I knew God loved mankind and I knew He wanted to rescue my soul, but actually to love me? What, me? The girl who is sometimes clumsy? Yes, me. What? The girl who forgets really important things (including later in life her wedding anniversary and parents' assemblies at my son's school)? Yes.

Me, the girl who loves nothing more than going home, getting into her pyjamas and snuggling up on the sofa with a hot cup of tea? Yes! He loves the real me!

I think sometimes we know God loves us when we're at what we may consider to be our best moments. But guess what, He loves you in your hidden and quiet moments too. He loves you. And when you and I really begin to grasp this, there's a quiet confidence that starts to arise. When we realise His love is towards us at all times, we begin to see differently, talk differently and live differently.

It was a slow journey of intimacy with God for me. But that increasing awareness of His love led to an increased confidence that was to help me in some of the bigger decisions I've had to take.

Books and The Beatles

Dad loved his books. His favourite author was A.W. Pink, so we had quite a reformed theological upbringing. Dad always had his head in a book. Often when the rest of us were watching TV, he'd take a book from the bookcase, sit on his spot on the sofa, and quietly read.

It developed within me a love for books as well. I remember numerous trips to the library as a family. One time, Dad took me and my middle sister, Wendy. He could be a bit of a joker so, for fun, he suggested we pretend to be tourists.

Tourists in Rotherham. Maybe a bit of an oxymoron.

We pretended to speak in another language. For me and Wendy, it was a kind of made up French, but I'm pretty sure my dad was speaking in tongues!

Books weren't my only love. Despite having been born after The Beatles had broken up, I loved them. I played their albums at every opportunity. I would constantly talk about them at school – by now I'd moved to Wingfield Comprehensive School. My maths teacher at school, Malcolm Fox, was aware of my love for The Beatles. In addition to teaching maths (my least favourite subject), he also took music classes. I remember him encouraging me in my singing, to such an extent that he took me and a few others to residential homes to perform.

His big surprise, though, was the trip. Along with two or three others, Mr Fox took us to Liverpool, the home of The Beatles. We went to the Cavern, the place they first performed, as well as many other sites in the city. I was so excited. These were my musical heroes and I got to visit their home city. It was a big thing for a girl who had hardly moved out of Rotherham!

Mablethorpe

It's not exactly true that I had hardly moved out of Rotherham. Family holidays were in Mablethorpe, Lincolnshire. And always Mablethorpe. We hired the same caravan each year.

Dad was such a gentleman. He insisted on always walking on the outside of the pavement, protecting us girls from any oncoming traffic. I remember one walk to the beach in particular. It had been raining hard the day before. There were puddles everywhere. I think the driver must have done it on purpose, but I remember vividly the car going through a puddle and Dad getting absolutely soaked by the spray. For Mum, my sisters and I, it was one of the high points of the holiday; quite hysterical. I'm not sure Dad thought the same way. He chased after the car, absolutely furious.

I have nothing against Mablethorpe. If you live there, you live in a good place. But to have your main summer holiday there year after year became a bit predictable. It was to escape from Mablethorpe that took me to my first mission adventure.

Chapter Two
The Escape Clause

With an early fascination for Africa and an increasing awareness that God was calling me, I was keen to get onto a mission – and maybe to escape the Mablethorpe holidays!

That opportunity came with a church mission trip to Sicily. I was only seventeen at the time and I felt that God had been preparing me to take this step – not least in dealing with my shyness.

Shyness

As a young teenager, I was incredibly shy. I remember Dad announcing one evening that I would be singing with my two sisters at next Sunday's church meeting. I was petrified. I ran up the stairs to my room and cried. It wasn't as if I was going to have to do too much – Donna, my oldest sister, would be taking the lead and all I had to do was to sing background vocals. Nevertheless, I was so worried about the event. My shyness was almost crippling. Despite that, we managed the event well enough and, looking back, maybe Dad was aware of my need to overcome any 'stage fright'.

Those early outings really did give me confidence and I became more of an accomplished singer through my teen years. At the age of twelve, we moved as a family to New Life Church, Rotherham, and through the pastoral care and encouragement of the pastor, John Andrews, I would regularly sing in the evening meetings. I was particularly attracted to the songs of Jaci Velasquez, and I would listen for hours to her albums, memorising the words and working out the basic guitar chords. Her song 'On My Knees' is still a favourite to this day.

Sadly, when I was pregnant with Josiah, somehow my voice changed and my singing is no longer as good as it was.

Youth Camp

'Mum, Dad, the youth are going camping; please can I go?'

'Yes, we know. But it's at the same time as our holiday in Mablethorpe.'

I was well aware of this. And part of me wanted to go just to get out of the Mablethorpe experience. I was wise enough not to say that to Mum and Dad – and bless them, they were happy enough for me to go with the youth group.

I was fourteen at the time, and the camp was one of those moments in time when you know God has worked in your life in a special way.

There were quite a few of us from New Life Church, Rotherham. We were joining a larger group of young people from a number of churches and were camping at Robin Hood's Bay on the coast near Whitby in Yorkshire.

I loved it. The camping, the walks, the fun with friends. And the boys. When you're fourteen years old, boys are important. Hannah, my friend from our previous church, was with me, and she was interested in one boy in particular. We arranged to sit with him and his friends on the Friday night, the plan being we would then all go out for a walk afterwards and Hannah and the boy could clinch the deal with a kiss! I rather spoilt it . . .

As the meeting progressed, I was more and more aware that God was at work. I sensed His presence. I knew that I needed to be baptised in the Holy Spirit.

I'd been seeking this baptism in the Spirit for some time, but nothing had happened back at our home church. I'm not sure I had been in a good place for God to move in that way. I had been bullying a girl called Rachel at school, and quite obviously living an entirely different life in my school hours to those spent at home or at church.

There were two sets of girl gangs you wanted to belong to at school: the very beautiful set, or the very cool set. I wasn't in the beautiful category, so I worked hard to be in the cool set. The price was a certain degree of nastiness that was required for me to fit in – and this had outworked itself in bullying poor Rachel. I had worked hard to be funny, always making jokes. And making Rachel the butt of nearly every joke had worked for me. I was well and truly part of the cool gang.

Being on a youth camp, in a different environment, really helped. I knew I had to change. I knew I had to live for Jesus every moment of every day. I couldn't be a different person at school. As the talk progressed that night, there was a deepening conviction of my need to change and of God touching me through the Holy Spirit.

Baptism in the Spirit

By now, part way through the meeting, I was feeling completely convicted by my behaviour towards Rachel. So much so, I made a vow to God.

'Lord, I'm so sorry for what I've been doing. Please forgive me for the way I have treated Rachel. I promise that just as I have publicly mocked her, I will publicly apologise to her when we're back at school.'

Immediately God met me. I felt a powerful anointing flow through me. I knew what it was. I knew God had just baptised me in the Spirit. I was so affected that I did the most unusual thing for me. Part way through the preaching that was still progressing, I got to my feet and started to speak out in tongues. The words were bubbling away inside me and just had to come out. So they did! I knew enough to know that you weren't meant to interrupt the preaching, but I felt such an overwhelming love for God at that moment, it seemed the only thing I could do.

It was dramatic. And it was life changing.

Hannah was not impressed. I had just ruined her Friday night walk by being all spiritual! Thankfully we were close enough friends for her to forgive me.

There was further forgiveness needed of course. I was true to my promise to God and at the first opportunity publicly apologised to Rachel at school. She didn't receive it too well, and I don't blame her – I had been horrid to her for nearly two years.

But the changes in me were lasting. I no longer felt my need for identity through the cool gang and, over a period of time, I found a whole new friendship group. Interestingly the girl who was the leader of the cool gang remained a friend – she was impressed by what I had done.

That moment at Robin Hood's Bay changed my life. There was a new boldness, a new certainty in who I was in Christ. I knew I had made the best of decisions. No more compromise. No more living two lives. I wanted to be all I could be for Jesus. I gave Him all and, by God's grace, I have continued over the years to give everything to Him.

Speaking Words of Life

How about you? As you read these words, what is your response? Is there compromise in your life? It's time to respond, to speak out, to declare that what God has for you in your life is the best. Anything less than God's best is a lesser life lived.

When Ezekiel spoke to the valley of dry bones (Ezekiel 37), he was obeying God's command. God chose Ezekiel to speak the words. He turned the solution to the problem back into the hands of Ezekiel. God said to Ezekiel, 'You speak hope! You speak life!' The miracle was in Ezekiel's own mouth.

And we know the story – as Ezekiel spoke, flesh came onto the dry bones. Breath came into the bodies. There was new life.

In the same way, the miracle is in your mouth today. God longs to do miracles in impossible situations. And He chooses to do it through you. He is choosing your mouth, your hands, your heart. As you speak out, breath comes into situations that seemed to be dead. New life instead of dead bones.

So speak! Declare an end to compromise. Decide to wholly follow Christ. If, like me, there was a need to ask forgiveness to obtain that freedom, do so. Be courageous. Speak boldly.

What do we need to speak? The Word of God is a good starting point. My friend Helen Roberts was diagnosed with cancer that appeared to be incurable, but a member of her church spoke life over her. As he prayed, he used verses from the Bible to speak that life.

If you don't feel you have enough of the Word of God in you, enough that comes to mind in those situations, let me encourage you to read the Bible regularly so that God's Word is *in* you. There are many Bible plans out there. One that helped my friend Helen was a study developed by Wayne Cordeiro in *The Divine Mentor*, using the acrostic 'SOAP'. It stands for 'read a Scripture, Observe, Apply, Pray'. We study a passage. Then we observe the content. We apply it to our situation. And we pray for the results. It's simple and it works.

Whatever study you choose, read the Word of God regularly. It gives you the words of life to speak into impossible situations and to see God's results. Today, my friend Helen is cancer free.

The Escape Clause from Mablethorpe

'Mum, Dad, the church is asking for volunteers for a mission trip to Sicily. Can I go? Please?'

'Yes, we know about it. But it's at the same time as our holiday in Mablethorpe.'

I smiled. This was becoming a regular conversation. Another escape from Mablethorpe beckoned.

'Well, alright. You'll need to get your own money together – and we'll miss you at Mablethorpe!'

And there it was. My first mission trip. Despite being aware of God's call on my life for mission, the main motive was the escape clause from our family holiday, to avoid boring Mablethorpe. Looking back, those holidays don't seem too boring now, but at the age of seventeen they were! I had a call to save the world, but at that stage, I just wanted to see the world.

The Sicily trip was a success and it whetted my appetite for more. So when there was an invite the next year to join a mission to Romania, I jumped at it. The situation in Romania at the time was pretty dire. With the fall of Communism some years earlier, the country had opened up and had exposed to the world the appalling cruelty to orphans and disabled children. Our church, along with many others, responded to the needs.

On this occasion we were based in Timişoara, near the western border of Romania, close to Serbia and Hungary. We were working with local churches, caring for a number of orphanages. I was posted to the baby unit of one of these.

It was a privilege to serve and help those children. As I reached out to them, I felt God reaching out to me again and reminding me of that call to Africa He had put on my life as a little girl.

It was on a day off, as I was out walking with my friend Becky Fox, that I felt I heard God speaking to me. We set off from the town and in a short time we were in the countryside. Such beautiful scenery. The trees blowing in the breeze. The summer sunshine touching the flowers as they reached upwards. By the time we got to our destination – a lake a couple of miles out of town – I was in a thoughtful and reflective mood.

We sat by the lake. As we did, in a way that was new to me, I felt I heard God directly speaking to me. I felt He was telling me that as part of my call I would start and run orphanages. That there would be children's homes established through my serving Him.

It was a complete shock – not least because it was not what I had wanted or expected with regard to mission. I had been imagining something more dynamic and evangelistic. But that voice was as clear to me as my friend Becky talking to me that same day. It seemed even more obvious that it was God talking to me because I simply would not have chosen that route. And because of that, the anticipation of God leading me in that new direction grew.

I was excited. This was a fulfilment of God's earlier promises. As soon as we got back home, I began to tell everyone what God had said. In my naïvety, I expected God to begin to open doors immediately. But it wasn't like that. Doors didn't open for me despite my desperate praying.

There was preparation still to be done in my life before I was ever to get on a flight to Africa.

Chapter Three
Encounter

Back home after the Romania trip, I was excited. God had called me. The doors would open. Orphanages would be built.

But the doors didn't open.

In fact, every time I pushed in terms of potential mission opportunities, there seemed to be a lock on the door. The harder I pushed, the more the door seemed to be permanently sealed.

Finishing my A levels at sixth form college, I had already decided I didn't want to pursue any further education and, on the basis that God was going to be calling me to serve internationally any day now, I took what I thought would be a temporary job.

'What are you going to do with your life?'

The job was with a debt-collecting agency.

I know. Not ideal perhaps for someone with a Christian faith, but I must say it toughened me up. Coming from such a happy and sheltered home, I hadn't really come across this other side of society. I'd never even heard much swearing.

On my first day I burst into tears. A woman was shouting at me over the phone, using the worst language I had ever heard. Someone else had to take over the call. But I'm grateful for that time. And it was quite a long time too. I joined at the age of eighteen in 1999 and only left in 2005.

Chris Dixie is a director there that I particularly remember. When things weren't opening up for me on the mission field, I began to lose my way a little bit. It was Chris who would challenge me.

'Becky, what *are* you going to do with your life?!'

He was right to ask. I had dreams of being a missionary, but they were not grounded. I had ideas of just going to another country and setting up there. I had no thoughts as to how, little understanding as to the finance needed. It was all 'in the clouds'. I wasn't really listening in to what God was saying to me.

That also meant that I was drifting. I was enjoying my work. Chris had promoted me and I liked the contact with the various financial institutions I worked alongside. But Chris could see I wasn't satisfied.

What was I to do with my life?

God Moment

I saved up all my annual leave for mission trips. One was to Colombia, working with David Taylor, a friend from Hull. I had vague ideas that God may be calling me to Guatemala, so a Latin America mission made sense to me. It was the trip after that one though, in 2004, when I went on a short-term mission to Mississippi in the United States with some of my local church, that God met me in a special way.

It was only after I'd signed up to go on this trip that I learned that we were also going to visit the church in Brownsville, near Pensacola, where a so-called revival had been taking place. I wasn't very happy about this! Dad had not really been in favour of the various 'revivals' we heard about from time to time, mainly happening in North

America, and maybe this had rubbed off on me a bit. Hence, I tended to avoid 'revival meetings' of all types.

By this time, our home church was in Wath upon Dearne (nowadays known as the Father's House Church), just north of Rotherham. Peter Morris was the pastor, a lovely godly man. The same could not be said about his renegade son, at least as far as I was concerned. Nathan Morris had been a wild young man. But God has ways of working with the most unlikely people and, some months before the mission trip, Nathan had found his way back to Christ with his life radically changed as a result.

It seemed unfair to me that this young man who had been so far away from God should now be so close to God! How could it be right for him to have such an obviously close walk with God after such a short time, when I'd been a faithful Christian for years and had no such closeness? There was no doubt about the change – Nathan had such a hunger and passion for God.

It was so annoying!

And it was with some further annoyance that I found that Nathan had also signed up for the same mission trip.

The annoyance didn't last though. As I chatted to Nathan at the beginning of the mission trip, I found myself longing for what he had found. It was a God moment for me. As I talked to Nathan, I felt God speaking to me loud and clear. I heard Him prompting me. What if, after all these years of serving God, there was more? What if God wanted to love me as a father loves a child, not just as a master loves a servant? The more I talked to Nathan, the more I began to realise I had only touched the surface of the relationship Father God wanted with me. I prayed:

'Lord God, I want what Nathan's got. I want that! I want the passion that Nathan has so obviously got. I want that passion I have seen in my own dad through the years. Lord, please, will you help me? Will you do something in me?'

The Brownsville Car Park

By the time we got to the church in Brownsville where the revival had happened, I was so hungry. But the revival itself had come and gone. Starting back on Father's Day in 1995, it lasted through to the early 2000s, but the original revivalists, Steve Hill and John Kilpatrick, had both moved on by now. Tommy Tenney was speaking on the day we were there.

It was a great talk – on the book of Esther – but nothing much seemed to happen, at least not to me. As the meeting came to an end, it was with a sense of disappointment that I left the auditorium. I was having an internal conversation with God as I pushed through the double doors, out into the car park.

'Well, Lord, maybe this is as good as it gets?'

As we walked towards the cars, my mind was by now set upon the promised cheeseburger we were being offered at Denny's restaurant. But there in front of us was a group of interns from the Brownsville church. They were the last group of people I wanted to talk to! Some of them were 'manifesting' in the Spirit: some shaking, others shouting 'wow' at seemingly inappropriate moments as they talked to us. Their team leader was Dr Sandy Kirk, and among their number was an English girl called Mary whom I had chatted to earlier.

'Can we pray for you?' asked Sandy.

'Sure,' said my friends.

I held back. I was tired by now and the thought of the approaching cheeseburger was larger in my mind than the thought of any further prayer.

The interns went right through the whole of the team from the UK, praying for each – but they missed me out.

'Well,' I said, 'you may as well pray for me as well.'

What an attitude! Looking back now, I wonder that God would pay the least attention to me. I really was not in a good place at that point.

They gathered round me. Mary placed her hands on my head.

I was well aware of the 'falling down' bit. I had observed it many times. People prayed for you and you felt somehow obliged to respond by gently falling backwards into someone's arms. At least, that was my view. I had never experienced it and had always resisted it. So, I was not about to 'oblige' this set of interns with anything dramatic.

What happened next was totally unexpected.

As Mary's hands touched my head, I began to laugh hysterically. What was I doing?! I couldn't stop it. I slid down to the floor, laughing louder and louder. What was God doing to me?

Down on the floor, I laid still. After what seemed to be a couple of minutes, I tried to get up.

It wasn't a couple of minutes. The team later told me I had been on the ground for over an hour. An hour! Wow. I had no idea. No idea either as to what God had been ministering to me over that hour, or what the interns had been praying over me.

As I tried to get up, I found I couldn't move. My arms and legs simply wouldn't respond. Some of the guys on the team lifted me up. They had to slide me into the minivan as if, as one of them described it later, they were sliding a loaf of bread into an oven.

I felt embarrassed. This was me! I didn't do things like this. I tried to apologise to the team.

And it was then that I realised I couldn't talk either. I was a bit freaked out by this, wondering for a moment whether I had had a stroke or something. But no, the peace that I felt meant it could only be God.

Back home I had been a somewhat opinionated young woman regarding the things of God. I remember a friend in our church groaning deeply in a meeting and me saying to myself, 'That's definitely not God. That's just her making noises and seeking attention!'

Imagine my extreme embarrassment, then, as I began to groan in just the same way in the back of the minibus. It was a groan, an aching deep within me. It is hard to explain except to say that I guess it's the kind of groaning Paul refers to in his letter to the church in Rome:

'Likewise the Spirit helps us in our weakness. For we do not know what to pray for as we ought, but the Spirit himself intercedes for us with groanings too deep for words' (Romans 8:26).

This groaning went on for some time. I couldn't even speak to apologise.

Over the following days, I realised something dramatic had happened to me. I fell in love with Jesus. There's no other way of saying it. I fell in love with my Lord in a way I didn't know was possible. He met me. He met me in my need. He met me when I was thinking of cheeseburgers. He met me when I was judging others.

And He loved me.

Never the Same

That was the day it all changed. That was the day I found a love that has lasted. Sure, I was a Christian before then, but one who somehow felt that I needed to serve God, to be doing things for Him all the time. Now I know. It's not to do with service. It's not to do with trying harder. It's love. I love Him. He loves me. Such a deep, deep love.

My life changed from that point. It started a whole new journey for me of seeking Him for who He is. Not for what I could gain. Not for what I could give. Just to be with Him.

I had been content with where I was at. I was accustomed to my way of living the Christian life. I didn't realise there was more.

In the Bible, in Numbers 32, the story is told of the tribes of Reuben and Gad. They reached the Promised Land, but they became content with the lands they were travelling through just before they were to cross over the Jordan River. It was good land. But it wasn't the Promised Land. God was angry with them for their lack of zeal, for missing out on all He was promising them.

Let me encourage you to have a holy discontent! Don't settle for what is there in front of you. Seek God. Seek His purposes for you. Don't settle for 'good enough' when God has so much more.

There is a mountain climb in the Alps that is often used for business corporate away days. It's an easy climb and the teams usually make it to summit within the day, before being taken down the mountain to celebrate their success.

Half way up the trail there is a small alpine restaurant. Teams reach there at lunchtime and stop for a snack and a cup of coffee or hot chocolate before continuing. But the thing is, so many that reach there, stop there. Over half of each business party out on this particular corporate challenge choose to stay in the restaurant! They are content with their achievement, they are appreciating the warmth, they like the view out of the window. And they never complete the climb.

We have a mountain to climb. Each of us. Challenges, things we need to overcome. Will we climb, or will we become satisfied and stop half way up?

The Bible tells of the story of Caleb. One of the spies sent by Moses to spy out the Promised Land, he brought a good report (Numbers 13:30). But others persuaded the Israelites that the land was too hard to take. The result was a forty-year walk through the wilderness until that generation had died out – all except Caleb and Joshua, who had spoken in faith of God's promises.

We then read of Caleb, now in the land, asking Joshua for the hardest part of that land – the area where giants had been seen. The exact mountain that had caused the Israelites to disbelieve. And at the age of eighty-five he took the mountain and defeated the giants.

Like Caleb, we need to keep our eyes focused on the Promised Land. We need to cry out to God, as Caleb did, 'Give me this mountain!' (Joshua 14:12).

As you read the words in this chapter, why not pray with me now:

'Lord Jesus, I don't want to be content with anything less than Your best for my life. I don't want to live a 'good enough' life. I want the best; a life that glorifies You. Please help me to have a holy discontent for anything less. I choose to climb the mountain. I choose to make myself vulnerable, to receive all You would give me, every Holy Spirit encounter You have for me. I choose to encounter You. Amen.'

Chapter Four
The Bamboo Hut

The weather was cold and damp. So were my spirits that day. Back home, in January 2005, I sat next to my friend Becky Torr as the church prayer meeting went on. And on.

The Flyer

I'd lost concentration a while back – and it was obvious that Becky had too. She was flicking through her Bible, looking at the various bits of paper that had become lodged between the pages. One was a flyer. Becky lifted it out of her Bible and showed it to me.

I read the contents, advertising a missions school, and said to Becky, 'I'm going to go!'

I was joking.

But God wasn't.

As soon as I said it, I felt a prompt from the Holy Spirit that I *was* actually to apply.

The flyer was advertising a Bible school in Mozambique with the well-known Christian leader Heidi Baker. At this stage I had never been to Africa, and my appreciation of Heidi and her ministry had not been positive.

I had first encountered Heidi on a DVD that my mum had given me. Mum had thought it was great and wanted me to watch the talk given at a conference in the UK. But a few minutes into the DVD, I felt I had to turn it off.

I was watching Heidi's talk before my Brownsville experience and as far as I was concerned, the moment she started 'manifesting', as I called it – shaking and twitching as a result of the work of the Holy Spirit as I now know – I didn't want to see more. It was showing off. It was drawing attention to herself. That was the end of it.

A short trip to Toronto soon after the Brownsville visit began to change my mind. I had now had my experience of meeting God in the car park and as the guest speaker was announced, I realised that this time I would be enjoying the whole of a talk from Heidi. I began to appreciate the depth of her relationship with the Lord and her love for the lost and marginalised in society.

So my response to the flyer was positive. But I was still just joking with my friend.

The Holy Spirit prompt meant that the application went off and in May that year I took my first flight to Africa. I later learned that there had been thousands of applicants and only two hundred selected, so I felt privileged to be there.

Life at the centre was not easy. There were no Western trappings. Forty or so to each dormitory. We had to dig our own pit latrines. We were required not just to attend lectures, but to work practically on the base as well, digging building foundations, setting up bamboo fences. I soon learned that my skills were not directed towards fence building!

The food was a bit of a challenge too. Plain boiled rice and plain boiled fish. Fresh bread for breakfast, but if you were at the back of the queue you got yesterday's bread – which would be rock hard. You learned to be on time for breakfast.

We had to share three bathroom cubicles between two hundred of us. The place was so dusty. On more than one occasion, I thought I had developed a bit of a sun tan, only to find it came off once I applied a wet-wipe.

Being so close together in the dormitories, you quickly learned to cope with each other. Better than that, we soon became friends. Very few had come to this mission opportunity with others, so we all started out on our own, and by the end of the three months we were firm friends.

Early Rising

Anyone that knows me will tell you I like my sleep. I'm not an early riser and because of that, I tend to spend time reading the Bible in the evening rather than in the morning.

But for my time in Mozambique that changed. Physically speaking, I don't know why that changed – the time difference compared to home wasn't significant, so it wasn't a body clock thing.

Every day I found myself waking at four in the morning. And I'd be wide awake too. Normally I need a couple of cups of coffee to get me moving, but in Mozambique I was simply awake so bright and early! I made the assumption it must be a 'God prompt' and therefore responded accordingly by taking time out with Him. Lectures didn't start until 9.00 a.m. so I had plenty of time.

Each day I would wrap a *capulana* around me – a brightly coloured strip of fabric worked in the style of a sarong – creep out of the dormitory and head down to the beach. Iris Ministries, the organisation that Heidi heads up, is based in Pemba. It's a beautiful place, right next to the white sands and palm trees that reach out into the sleepy waves of the Indian Ocean. Idyllic at any time of day but at four in the morning, I had the place to myself.

This lasted a while, but I found that by 5.00 a.m. the street vendors were active. If they saw a visitor on the beach, they would make a beeline for them, wanting to sell their homemade products and souvenir trinkets.

I didn't want to be rude, but I'd come to the beach at the invitation of the Holy Spirit, so needed time to be on my own.

'Lord, what am I to do? I feel this is You waking me up every morning, but I need to be alone with You.'

The Secret Place

With two hundred students on the site the place was crowded. Plus numbers of children being cared for. Plus staff. Plus local people helping to run the place. How could I ever find a quiet place?

One morning I walked in a different direction, behind the staff accommodation and through to their car park. There it was. By the side of the car park, set away from all the buildings. A little bamboo hut. Round bamboo walls. A straw roof. Crazy paving for the floor.

For the three months I was with Iris Ministries it became *my* bamboo hut! I made sure I didn't tell anyone else about it. It was my secret place with God. I got to know every piece of that paving as I sat on the floor and prayed. The only person who ever went past was the gardener watering the plants. I loved it. It was as if my Father had personally found me my quiet hideaway: a place I could use without being disturbed, a place I could use for my personal worship and private study. A time with God. Precious. Alone.

Four in the morning became my most treasured moment in the day. I couldn't wait to get up and to spend time with my Father. Because I was away, normal life had been set aside. If it were possible

I was falling more and more in love with Him. Just to be in His presence. To quietly sing, to read the Psalms, to reflect on Jesus' love for me. These moments stand out even today as some of the most precious in my life.

All I would carry with me was my Bible and a notebook. It was there that I learned to journal, to write down my thoughts and prayers. I have the journal to this day, full of cherished promises from God, with prayers and psalms written to Him from the bottom of my heart.

It was as a result of these times with God that I was able to say 'yes' to Him more easily. I heard Him more loudly. I knew His heart. I was ready to embrace the journey God had for me and I could hear even the whispers of the Holy Spirit as He laid that journey out for me.

In the Waiting

I found God in the waiting. For all of us, with the pressures of life and the speed at which we travel through that life, it is easy to miss the waiting. But these times with God are precious. In fact, I'd say they are essential.

Too often, we wish away our everyday lives trying to reach some future destination, the place we think we are supposed to be. We rush so much, we miss the everyday opportunities God puts into our everyday path. We miss His prompts. We miss His words of preparation.

For all of us, there will be seasons of waiting. Seasons of preparation. We may think we are ready, but often God puts an amber light in front of us, rather than a green one. It's not that we have missed what He wants for us, but we often think it is for 'now' when in fact God is saying 'wait and let Me prepare you for the journey'.

The prophet Isaiah says, 'He made my mouth like a sharp sword; in the shadow of his hand he hid me; he made me a polished arrow; in his quiver he hid me away' (Isaiah 49:2).

So often I feel like the arrow. I am being pointed in the right direction. I know what I have to do. I have a clear understanding of the task ahead of me. But at the crucial moment the archer pulls the arrow back. Instead of heading for my target, suddenly God is pulling me back and into His cheek as He stretches the bow.

It may seem like a backward moment. It may seem like the call God has for us is never going to happen. But see it for what it is. Our Father is pulling us back, into His cheek, into His protection. It's a precious time, a time of quiet and reflection. A time for Him to speak and encourage before we are sent out to the task ahead.

If we are not careful, in that moment of being pulled back we assume we must have done something wrong; we wonder if we have somehow been disobedient. But no. We are being brought close to the Archer's cheek – closer to God.

Waiting is a time to press in to God. We are not alone in our waiting. Joseph had to wait thirteen years before his dreams were fulfilled. David had to wait twenty-two years from being anointed king of Israel to it actually happening. There was a lot of sheep-tending to be done before the kingship.

We see so clearly that God is in the waiting with Joseph and David. They had to wait. They had to learn, to prepare for the task. And God was with them in that waiting.

Our identity is in God, not in what we do for God. He is with us in the waiting. The waiting is part of the journey too. Don't just keep looking ahead, longing for 'the day' to arrive. We are in the everyday with Him. He is with us in the waiting as much as the going.

Covenant

Each day with God in that bamboo hut was a time of waiting. There was an anticipation too. I expected God to speak, not just showing His love but showing me the big picture – what He was preparing me for. In fact I was having this rather forthright conversation with Him.

'God, anytime now is good! Whenever You want to speak. Whenever You want to meet me and show me a vision is fine with me!'

Nothing. Just nothing.

I studied each day, I had beautiful times with Him. But I was somehow expecting a special moment, a revealing word, a clarity of call . . . But it never came in that way.

I wrote these words in my journal: 'While I wait for Your gift, I want to give You my gift.' It was an expression of my heart. I would be faithful even if there was to be no technicolour moment of vision and direction.

As I wrote these words in my journal, the word that came to mind was 'covenant'. It wasn't a word I was used to – not one in my general vocabulary. If I spoke of my relationship with God, I would use words such as 'promise' or 'closeness'. 'Covenant' seemed to mean more than that. I felt it was important, so I wrote it into my journal directly after my words on giving my own gift to Him. I wrote:

'Today I come into covenant with You. When You saved me, that was You giving me Your life. Lord, have I ever really given You my life? I choose not to put You in a box. I don't just want to give You my Sundays. Take it all, Lord. Take my whole life.'

We talk, as Christians, about giving God control. But do we really do that? In the bamboo hut that day I gave God a gift. I gave Him myself. Unreservedly. Completely, as far as I knew how. I said, 'Lord, that's my covenant with You. Do with me whatever You want, send me wherever You want. Whatever that looks like, have all of me.'

I finished praying and began again to write the words in my journal. As I finished, I looked up to the straw roof, and there was a frog. So I wrote, 'With the frog as my witness, today I come into a covenant relationship with You.'

As I put down my pen and closed the journal, I was expecting more. Surely that was the moment for God to move? For His vision to be declared for me? But no, nothing.

I shrugged. Time for lectures anyway.

Lectures

Most of our lectures were in a big green-and-white tent. As I walked in that morning, I saw that the lecturer was Ian Ross. Ian had been part of the teaching team at the Toronto church where the Holy Spirit had been outpoured from the early 1990s onwards.

He looked up at us all and said, 'Before I start this morning, I just feel heavily on my heart that God is speaking to some of you and that He wants to give some of you a gift today.'

Well, that had my attention!

He went on, 'I feel God is speaking about covenant.'

I nearly jumped off my chair.

'A covenant is like a marriage. It has to be two-way. Both have to commit, both covenant together.'

I can't remember the lecture that followed. I was overawed with what God had just done. It was as if Ian had read my journal, written just an hour before the lecture. God was so good! I now had a human witness, not just a frog in the top of the bamboo hut.

At the end of the lecture I went up to Ian with one of the strangest sentences I bet he's ever heard: 'Ian, you are better than a frog!'

He did look at me rather strangely.

Assaulted

Much as my time at Pemba was a precious experience, there was a moment there that over the years I have tried to forget. But it would not be right to pretend it didn't happen, to wish it away.

We occasionally had days off and for me, as an English girl, this was an opportunity to go to the beach and top-up my tan. In Mozambique, culture dictates that you should not uncover your knees – to do so would be to announce to others that you were a prostitute.

Looking back I should have known better, but I wanted that tan so I had rolled up my *capulana* and, in that state, I walked down the beach. There were starfish there like I'd never seen before. In fact I have never seen anything like them since. Vibrant colours. Beautiful shades of red, green and blue, with so many shades in between. I was captivated by them, so did not see the man come up behind me.

As I was bending down, he lifted my *capulana* and pushed his body against me. I screamed, turned around and backed away. By now he had exposed himself.

I didn't know what to do, but caught in the corner of my eye the local beach café, the Dolphin. I figured if I could make it there, I would be safe. I also needed to be brave, and not to show fear. I shouted 'no' both in Portuguese and the local tribal language. But still he came towards me, exposed.

I walked as fast as I could without running. He followed. Thankfully, the café was not that far away and I ran in, pretty distressed by now. Two of the girls from the mission camp were there, having breakfast. Seeing the state I was in, they rushed over to me. Once the man saw that others were with me, he backed away and ran off down the beach.

My upbringing was sheltered. I have a loving family. I had hardly been out of Rotherham. So, to be assaulted in this way was such a shock. I prayed with the girls at the café and later phoned my friend Amanda to pray with her – I figured I couldn't phone Mum and Dad as to do so would have caused them to want to get on the next available flight.

It didn't quite end there. Looking back, I should have reported the man to the police, but I didn't. Two days later we were in our morning lectures in the big tent. These lectures are carried out in English and are just for the students. Part way through the lecture a man came in, clearly drunk, and sat down on a seat right in front of me. I wanted to scream. It was him. I felt a rise of anger and had to hold myself back from hitting him.

Meredith, one of the girls that had been at the café, saw what was happening and recognised the man. While the lecture progressed, Meredith came over to me, placed her hands on my head and began to quietly speak in tongues. All of the anger and all of the fear left me. It was immediate. So much so, I was able to go over to the man after the lecture and say to him, 'Jesus loves you.' He looked at me, surprised and taken aback. He stumbled out of the tent and I never saw him again, but I know that in a moment when he should have expected anger and retaliation, he was shown God's love. I pray he found it.

Fear had been replaced by compassion. It was God's doing.

As I write these words, I know that they will be read by many women who have faced similar moments in their lives. Where there is still fear or anger, where the issue is unresolved within you, where it is still torturing you – please seek help. Get other Christian friends to pray with you. Ask God to help you. Bring the moment out into the light of God's love. Allow Him to banish the fear and anger once and for all. Where God's light shines, darkness is defeated.

Going Home

Much of my time in Pemba had been about waiting. But eventually, for me, there was a going. An end to the three months and an end to those precious times in the bamboo hut.

The lectures during those three months were so precious too. Heidi in particular. But I remember a number of guest speakers – not least, Bill Johnson from Bethel Church, Redding, California. I was so fortunate to receive teaching from people like Heidi and Bill. The subjects we studied were pretty broad: Working Cross-Culturally, Languages, Medical Training, Theology and Intimacy with Jesus, to name just a few.

As I boarded the plane at Maputo International Airport, it was as if I had been away for years. I was changed. Much more assured in my walk with Christ. Far more certain as to my call. Clearer in my relationship with a Father who loved me. Precious times.

Chapter Five
Shaking Nations

Landing back in the UK and returning to Rotherham, I felt different. My experiences in the bamboo hut had changed me. I felt closer to God. I know He is always close to us, but for me I felt that closeness in a new way.

I needed to prepare for all God would have me do on the mission field. Despite there being no great 'direction' moments in Pemba, I was sure of the call and certain it would happen. With that in mind I decided I needed to pursue a career in nursing. I felt that this would be the best preparation I could give myself for what God wanted to do in the future. In the meantime, I reasoned I could return to my job in the debt-collecting agency which my boss Chris – the very same person who had challenged me to do something with my life – had kindly left open for me.

The Meal

I had arranged to meet Chris over a meal and to discuss how best to fit back into the business. I was excited to tell him of all that had happened. Although he didn't have a Christian faith, he was so supportive. I went through some of the highlights and then landed on my decision.

'So, I know that I need to become a nurse. That's my best preparation for what God has for me. I want to go to university and do a degree in paediatric nursing.'

'What do you mean, Becky? You're leaving?'

'Well, no, I'd like to come back for a while until I can sort out the nursing degree.'

Chris sighed.

'Becky, you've just put me in an impossible situation. I left the job open for you because you were coming back. But now you are telling me you're going. Your plan to be a nurse means it just wouldn't be right for me to take you back. How could I do that when it simply wouldn't be in the interests of the company?'

Silence.

I had just verbally signed my leaving certificate. Chris was right. I couldn't treat the job as a stop-gap until nursing. He needed someone who would be committed to the business. I was naïve, but at the same time I was thankful that I had been honest. Chris had been good to me, and I didn't want to repay him with a few months' work and with investment in my career on his part, only to then leave.

It did put me in a bit of a predicament though. How could I survive without a job?

My parents were not happy. How could I have been so silly as to let go of a well-paid job? And what were all these ideas about university? No one from our family had been to university, so the whole concept was alien to Mum and Dad. I had managed to get three very good A level passes at school, so there was enough there to get me to enrolment, but there was definitely a family tension at this time because of the choices I was making.

God knew of my predicament, of course, and He had things well under control. Mum and Dad came around to understanding my passion for mission, and I was able to take up a temporary call-centre job with a large company before going to university in May 2006, to Sheffield, in order to study paediatric nursing. Three years and one degree later, I was qualified.

With a specialism in children's nursing, I reasoned that I would soon be heading out onto the mission field in order to serve God as a full-time, long-term missionary. I was reading books about those who had gone before me with medical training such as David Livingstone and Amy Carmichael. I was excited – this was God's call for me. I just needed to hear from God as to the destination and off I would go.

Again, I was getting ahead of myself. God had other plans.

Dad

I've never known my dad to be defeated. Always whistling, often singing, he was such a powerhouse in our family. A supporter of all I was doing, even when he thought it unwise.

We first began to notice something was wrong around the time I started as a nurse. I remember one day getting a lift home from church from Dad as my car was in the garage. We started out well enough, but within a few minutes we were in the middle of an industrial estate. At first I thought Dad was taking some sort of short cut due to road works, but it became clear he'd gone completely the wrong way.

'Dad, what are you doing?' I said.

'Oh, I don't know. I don't know what I'm doing!'

At the time I laughed it off, but over the next few weeks it became clear something was seriously wrong. In fact, Mum had known for some time that Dad was struggling but had covered it over.

Dad was presenting signs of what might be Alzheimer's – a loss of memory, confusion, not thinking straight. As a trainee nurse at the time, I suggested he should go for tests. Mum and Dad cried. They had both suspected something like this but had not wanted to admit it.

The tests came back. It was Alzheimer's. Dad was only in his early sixties.

He died of pneumonia and complications from treatment related to Alzheimer's in May 2018. I had wanted him to go in a better way, something more glorious, with his family around him, but it wasn't to be.

My fondest memory of Dad is of his passion for Jesus. He was always reading – either the Bible or some sort of theology book. He so loved God. And now he is with Him.

Shake the Nations

By the mid-2000s, Nathan Morris had set up his own charity, Shake the Nations. This was his vehicle for an evangelistic and healing ministry, working with others to bring the message of Christ to those who did not know Him.

What had started as Saturday-night services in his dad's church had grown exponentially. People from all around the country started coming to the meetings, without them even being advertised. The success of these meetings led to Nathan accepting invitations to run gospel crusades in various parts of Africa.

It was then that Nathan approached me and asked if I would join him on one of the crusades.

To be honest, I had no real interest. My passion was to care for the poor, to set up children's homes and feeding programmes. I said to a friend around that time that I'd only really be interested in Nathan's crusades were there to be an element to them of caring for the poor.

My initial response to Nathan was to tell him that I would pray about it – the polite Christian way of saying to someone that you are not really interested!

'Okay, Becky, but do let me know.'

A week later I happened to see Nathan in town.

'Becky, have you thought any more about the Sierra Leone trip? I feel we need to work with the poor as well as preach the gospel. There seems to be a number of rubbish dumps around the poorer parts of the capital, Freetown, and I just feel you are the one to help with that.'

Well, that got my attention.

Sierra Leone

That visit to Sierra Leone was the first of many. But it was the one that sealed my call with an awareness that it was time to start.

All that was because of Felicity. A nine-year-old girl offering herself sexually because she thought that was the thing to do when someone bought you fifty-pence flip-flops.

When I was nine, I was just so naïve. I was playing with Barbie dolls at that age. Here was a girl, already broken by adults, coerced into sexual activity to stay alive.

I couldn't concentrate for a moment the rest of that evening. At the crusade meeting, I was still so taken up with what Felicity had said.

She and her friend Solomon were with us that evening at the crusade, following the events earlier in the day. They saw miracles; they saw the blind eyes of a man they knew open. And they found faith in Christ.

Two years later, I met Solomon again and asked about Felicity, but he had lost contact and had not seen her in over a year.

So I never saw her again. But if ever anyone travels to the city of Bo in Sierra Leone and meets a local called Felicity, ask her if she had a young woman once buy her pink flip-flops. And if she says 'yes', hug her and tell her that because of her story, thousands of lives have been changed.

Gunshots

That first visit to Sierra Leone was my non-negotiable moment with God. Because of Felicity, I knew not only that I was called but that I was to start. I no longer had any choice in the matter – I had to give my life for this. For the orphan. For the girls in the slave trade. For the poor and the destitute.

The trip wasn't without its challenges though – the first of which was before we even got on the plane. A lady in our church spoke to Nathan and said that she had seen in a vision two gunshots being fired on one of the rubbish dumps in Sierra Leone. Nathan had shared it with me and, to be honest, I had dismissed it as just scare tactics from the enemy.

But on the train journey to the airport, Nathan pulled out a letter from someone else – unknown to the first person – saying the same thing: two gunshots on a rubbish dump. This time I took it seriously.

The immediate response from me was not one of faith. The letter adding to the earlier message struck fear into my heart and cast doubt in my mind. I really struggled. To get one message might be seen as just someone a bit 'off' with a prophetic word, but two the same . . .

My long-term friend Amanda Marrow was with me. We were the two due to be heading-up the feeding programme on the dumps.

On that seemingly endless train journey from Rotherham to King's Cross London, we prayed. And we prayed.

Our decision was to go ahead. We chose not to share the words with anyone else on the team, but we would push through, and if (rather dramatically as we saw it at the time) the bullets were for us, so be it.

The Blue Container

'Sister Becky, this is for you.'

The pastor's wife stood in front of me with a big smile and an even bigger container. Bishop Abu Koroma had arranged for the pastor's wife and her team to prepare a rice dish. Packed in a blue container, there was enough rice to feed fifty people. I was excited. This was my very first step towards feeding the poor; the culmination of years of prayer, prophetic words and seeking God.

The location chosen was a derelict bus shelter and its surrounds. This was the home for numbers of amputees.

The civil war in Sierra Leone had been brutal. It was commonplace for rebel armies to take over towns and villages. The 'game' they played was to ask the child of the family whether daddy liked to wear long-sleeved or short-sleeved shirts. Depending on the child's answer, the soldiers would cut the father's arm off either at the wrist or the elbow.

The van came to a stop. Amanda and I began to organise the feeding programme for the day. In front of us were many of the amputees and their families. Because of the amputees' condition, it was almost impossible for them to get work, so they depended on charity.

The problem was there were a lot more than fifty. A lot more. Well over a hundred.

'What should we do, Amanda? They've come for food and we're preaching to them first. If there's no food after the preach, that's not going to reflect well on what we have said.'

'I don't know,' said Amanda. 'I think we have to feed them anyway and see how far we can get.'

That's what we did.

We spoke first, and a number in the crowd responded and gave their lives to Jesus Christ that day.

Then we distributed the rice. Amanda and I stood behind the table, ladling out the rice dish, which was mixed with meat and vegetables. And we kept on ladling.

At the end, one of the helpers asked whether we could give any leftovers to a family in one of the nearby houses who had been too ill to come.

'Of course,' I said, and began to scrape out the remains from the blue container. I was scraping the rice into an orange plastic washing-up bowl. The plastic bowl was far bigger than the blue container, yet when I had finished scraping out what was left, there was more in the bowl than appeared to have been left in the original container.

It was only then that I realised.

God had just done a miracle. Just as with the feeding of the five thousand in the Bible, God had met our needs and supernaturally grown the meal well beyond its original size. We had fed over a hundred with a meal for fifty – and had even more left over. I had actually preached on the feeding of the five thousand the day before at an orphanage, but I must admit, I had no expectation that God would do such a thing.

Amanda and I were astounded, almost shocked by what had happened. What a good God we serve, to give so generously to those with nothing.

For the rest of the trip we were just so excited! We saw many people respond to the gospel and saw some amazing healings, but the highlight remained that day at the derelict bus shelter.

In my head, what happened only happened to heroes like Heidi Baker, not to ordinary people like me.

There were no bullets either. If we had heeded the warning we would not have seen the miracles.

I remember eventually telling the team at the end of the trip about the bullets warning. As I was talking at the hotel, suddenly a balloon popped from a party that was taking place there. We jumped a bit more than we usually would for a balloon!

That event with the blue container changed my faith levels. Years later, as I hold invoices in my hand for building works at children's homes and refuges around the world, I always think back to a certain blue container. I picture it in my mind's eye – and I know that God will meet the need.

Good Life or Abundant Life?

Miracles such as the multiplication of the rice point to a God of abundance. He wants to bless us. He wants us to have all He has to give us in this life. But too often we settle for a good life rather than an abundant life, a safe life rather than stepping out of our self-imposed comfort zones to embrace the miraculous, to walk with God, to hear His voice and to obey His call.

Jesus says, 'I came that they may have life and have it abundantly' (John 10:10). As you read these words, let me encourage you to seek God's abundance in your life, that each of us will overflow with God's blessing for others.

45

Let's become discontent with breadcrumbs from the Father's table and desire whole loaves of bread from the One who holds the heavens open to bless His people (Deuteronomy 28:12).

I was asked on one occasion, early on in my mission work, to supervise communion in a small African church. The problem was that the congregation didn't have a lot of food. They were hungry. So when I went around with the bread at communion, they took great chunks of it – and the whole loaf had gone by the end of the first row.

How hungry are you? The enemy may try and send spiritual bullets to stop you, but you need to know God has a giant-sized blue container of blessings with your name on it.

Chapter Six
One by One: Two by Two

Back home I continued with my nursing training, but there were a number of conversations with Nathan about working with him. Nathan had realised that the compassion shown on the streets opened the door for preaching the gospel, so he was keen to continue with both. And he asked me to head up the compassion ministry. OneByOne was born.

Initially, while we were still part of Nathan's ministry, it was called 'Shake the Nations – One By One'. I would regularly take out teams to help Nathan, serving with the compassion ministries while he majored on the gospel and the evening healing crusades. The name OneByOne reflects my own passion for the ones lost and alone. I toyed with the idea of calling it 'Feed the Nations' because it fitted in with Nathan's overall charity, but I didn't want to be caught with a title that was only about one aspect of what we did.

It was my friend Laura Boyes (now my sister-in-law as well) who came up with the name when we were chatting on the phone. It felt right and was a really good reflection of my own heart for missions. It was clear to me that I had found what I was called to do and the name I should use. I'm not one for the big crowds. I love the one-to-one conversations. I want to stop for the one.

Attitude and Arrogance

Something else was happening at that time.

When I went on that first Sierra Leone mission, there was another member of the team working as Nathan's assistant. He'd been recently converted to Christ and seemed to be completely over the top. He seemed overly sure of himself – and to me he was definitely and quite simply a big-head with an attitude. His background was journalism, and I think this helped with his confidence in public situations. He always had a view and was not afraid to tell you what that view was. I interpreted that as arrogance.

If there's one thing I cannot stand it's arrogance. It's like a red rag to a bull for me. I like most people most of the time, but when they show arrogance, that's something else.

Consequently, I planned to avoid this man at all costs. I simply couldn't get on with him. I figured that the first team to Sierra Leone was big enough for me to be able to keep away from him.

His name was Matthew Murray.

Our first meaningful interaction – and first argument – came about because of suitcases. I was aiming to take as many clothes for children as our suitcases could carry. I'd been busy encouraging the team to take as little as possible for themselves in order to take more clothes for the compassion work.

At the same time, Matt had been asking the same people to take fewer clothes in order to fit in as many copies of 'decision cards' as possible. These were the cards we would be using at the evening crusade meetings and it was best we took them with us rather than rely on local printers.

Matt approached me.

'Becky, will you take some decision cards in your case please?'

'Well, before I answer that, will you take some kids' clothes in your case?'

'Oh no,' said Matt, 'I've not got room.'

'Well,' I said, maybe showing a little bit of the attitude I disliked in others, 'I haven't got room either.'

And I walked off.

Second Night of the Crusade

I managed to successfully avoid Matt on the flight over. My opinion of him had not changed, and by now, because I was being so 'stand-offish', he'd decided that I was arrogant, thinking that I thought he was not good enough to get to know me.

On the first night of the crusade, Nathan paired everyone up for ministry at the end of the evening. It didn't work too well as he paired up people of the same sex. We realised that it was better to pair up male and female as this allowed more ministry, rather than restricting pairs of the same sex to praying for people of the same sex.

On night two, everyone paired up as requested by Nathan. I was not quick enough in finding one of the men on the team that I could work with and, to my absolute horror, I found that there was only one male member of the team left . . . Matt.

At the end of that meeting we began to minister together to people coming forward for prayer. We saw a number of people healed. This led to my first positive thought about Matt – though not exactly a ringing endorsement, I decided Matt couldn't be too bad if people got healed when he prayed for them.

By the end of that first Sierra Leone trip, we were good friends. He was very much in the 'just friends' category though – I had already told God that I wanted a husband who was tall, dark and handsome (of course!) and with an Irish accent. I'm not sure why but I've always liked that accent.

Close Friend

Despite me viewing this as an entirely platonic relationship, I quickly found that Matt was becoming a really close friend. I found that I was able to share things with him that I wasn't even sharing with some of my close girlfriends.

And it wasn't long before he became my best friend.

By now I was working student placement shifts at the hospital, adding experience to the nursing education I was receiving with my college course. I'd come home after long fourteen-hour shifts to find Matt there waiting for me. And I'd be pleased to see him, despite just having worked such long hours.

One or two of my girlfriends asked me about our relationship, but I was quick to assure them it was an entirely good-natured friendship and we were absolutely 'just friends'. Maybe if I had allowed myself the thought, I might have guessed that, for Matt, this wasn't quite the case.

The testing point for me was when a former girlfriend of Matt's in the church broke up with her then boyfriend and started giving Matt some of her attention.

I started to feel jealous.

This was ridiculous! After all, I reasoned, we were only friends. Matt had no interest in me. Why on earth was I feeling like this? It was just Matt!

But it didn't get any easier. I hated that this girl was paying Matt so much attention. If I saw her talking to him at church, I'd go straight over and join in the conversation. My feelings were all over the place. What was all this about?!

As I lay in bed one Sunday night, I began to reassess my relationship with Matt. I loved everything about him. His passion for God. His crazy sense of humour. I even liked his jokes. Maybe there was more to this relationship than I was willing to accept . . .

After Church

As usual when I wasn't working, Matt and I would go back to one of our homes for coffee after the Sunday-evening service. This was just a week after I had been pondering our relationship and I couldn't help noticing that Matt was quieter than usual. We would normally talk for hours together, naturally enjoying each other's company, but this evening Matt looked a bit strained as he made me a cup of coffee at his house.

'So come on, Becky, what's happening?'

'What do you mean?' I asked nervously.

'You know what I mean. Becky, I need to tell you I love you. And I really don't think I can carry on like this, just being friends.'

Matt was being Matt. Straight to the point, decision made. I don't work like that. I need time to think about things. He agreed to give me a week to think it through.

I thought it through.

The next Sunday morning, I saw Matt already seated for the meeting. Going over to him, I gave him a kiss on the cheek, looked him in the eyes, and said 'Yes'.

We started dating that December 2006 and married in June 2008. My work with OneByOne was suddenly two by two.

Intimacy

This is one of the most important things you will read in this book. I love Matt. He's the person God planned for me to marry. He's my best friend and lover. He's fun to be with. I love him.

But my relationship with Matt and the intimacy of our marriage is only a shadow of how we can know our God. Let me explain.

Marriage is probably the closest relationship, naturally speaking, in terms of intimacy. At the time of writing this, I've been married for twelve years now to Matthew and I'm still discovering new things about him. We have lived together for the last 144 months and so I know certain things about him. I know he hates his face being touched first thing in the morning, I know he hates it when I put my freezing-cold feet on his nice warm legs at night. I know he loves to have his egg yolks runny and his chicken seasoned with certain spices. And because we've lived together for a while now, he knows how I function way better after a coffee in the morning and how I love to receive chocolates over flowers any day of the week. (Any day of the week, Matt . . .) There are additional things we know about each other that other people will never know, because they're intimate and private details.

We have quite a big circle of friends with whom we love going out for meals and coffees but there are certain parameters to what we will tell them. We also have a small number of very close friends with whom we share many things, but still there are some things that Matt and I will only talk about when we're alone together.

You see, intimacy opens access to areas that are otherwise not permitted.

The wonder of all wonders for me is that God welcomes us, normal people like me and you, into an intimate relationship with him.

Daniel describes it as a God who reveals mysteries (Daniel 2:28), Amos describes it as revealing secrets (Amos 3:7), whilst the book of Revelation talks about a hidden manna (Revelation 2:17).

There are different thoughts about what this manna refers to; it could be wisdom, or revelation, or the way God provides for us not just materially but spiritually on this journey of life. It's clear that God has things He wants to share with those who draw close to Him.

We're invited into a relationship that isn't distant or formal. We're invited as children of God into the inner chamber. How privileged we are to have such access, but for some reason many of us don't go this deep. We often stay in the outer courts, we come into the temple area but not many venture into the Holy of Holies or even the inner courts.

Don't stay outside. Come in. Come in to an intimate relationship with Him. Jesus has made a way.

As we find that intimate place with our God, we find that we become more confident in all areas of life. We know who loves us most, and that helps us love others, whether that be our spouse or the person queuing at the food bank.

Our strength of relationship with God makes us secure. It's how I can do what I do with OneByOne. And for you, as you read these words, I pray your intimacy with God will be such that whatever you face, you will know that He is with you.

Chapter Seven
God With Us

The Saturday-night meetings at Wath were continuing as Shake the Nations became a higher profile Christian organisation in the UK. It was clear God was with us. We knew His blessing. These meetings were a platform for the support we needed on mission. Nathan encouraged me to establish a formal charity for the OneByOne work in order to better manage the finances.

From 2006 through to 2009, I was actively involved in three or four international trips each year with Nathan and Matt. We went to Sierra Leone five times during this period, with other trips to Kenya, Tanzania, Nigeria and India.

We developed a format for the main crusade meetings when we were travelling. After the initial salvation call, where we continued to see many thousands accept Jesus Christ as their Saviour, we would then pray for the sick. On one side of the platform we would deal with those needing deliverance and on the other, those seeking healing.

Miracles

It was a blessed time. We sought God for healing and saw many miracles. One early experience for Matt and I as we prayed for the sick related to a nineteen-year-old boy. He was deaf and dumb, and had been from birth. As we prayed for him, he suddenly jumped up, almost knocking Matt over. Unable to speak, he began to point to his ears, frantically looking around. We realised that he was beginning to hear for the first time as he sought out the source of the booming sounds coming from the speakers on the stage.

Matt saw a lady get up out of a wheelchair and walk – he had been specifically praying for 'walking miracles'!

A blind Imam from the local mosque came to one of the meetings. He was there to check up on who from the mosque was attending the Christian meetings, but God had other plans for him. As he stepped onto the field where we were holding the meetings, God opened his eyes. This miracle caused considerable bewilderment back at the mosque!

On the Steps of a Mosque

Our 2007 trip to Sierra Leone was memorable for another reason. By now we were well into our feeding programmes and near the end of the trip, travelling from one town to another. We had a lot of rice left over from the feeding programmes and decided to give it away as we went. I wanted to reach the smaller villages – again a reflection of my desire to meet people one by one. It seemed so easy to drive past these numerous villages and not stop.

The intention was to find the chief in each village and present him with bags of rice to give to the villagers. At the same time, we would gather a crowd and briefly preach the gospel before going on to the next village.

At one particular village it was more difficult. There wasn't an obvious gathering place – there was no market square or community building, which were the places we looked for when we got to a village.

All I could see was a large mosque with big steps in front of it. Amanda was with me again, as was Paul Morris, Nathan's uncle. I said to the two of them, 'What do you think, guys? There's only the mosque here. Shall we stand on the steps?'

We did. With our driver as the translator, I began to share a simple gospel message. I must admit, I was expecting trouble. This was a Muslim village and we had the effrontery to be preaching Jesus on the steps of their mosque. But they were quiet and listening. I even asked my driver at one point whether he was accurately translating what I was saying. He assured me he was.

Right there on the steps of the mosque, the message of Jesus' salvation was preached. And right there, numbers in the crowd that had gathered prayed a prayer of salvation, asking Jesus to change their lives.

Sometimes we have to be bold. Sometimes we have to stand on the steps in the hardest of places with the greatest of challenges. And why not? God is with us. Will we stand?

The Angel with the Mystery Electrics

The missions were not without challenges. We were threatened with knives in our meetings in India and we often received verbal threats wherever we went. But God always came through.

On one of the Sierra Leone trips, we were travelling in a convoy of cars from one location to another. I was once again with my friend Amanda. The other cars were ahead of us, and they failed to see that our car was having problems. Eventually we ground to a halt and the driver lifted the bonnet. After some time checking various leads and plugs, he looked up with a pained expression on his face.

'It's the electrics. An electrical fault. One of the wires has burned out – it's a small part that's broken, but it's hard to get. I'm not sure we will be able to do anything for now. It's too late to try and walk back to the town. We need to find somewhere safe to stay.'

We looked around. Dusk was approaching – and in Africa, the sun goes down rapidly. There were no houses in sight and ahead only dense woodland. Not a place for a couple of English missionaries to become stranded. It wasn't helped by the apparent anxiety of our driver. At one point, as it began to get dark, he recommended that Amanda and I duck down below the back seat of the car so we wouldn't be seen. Be seen by whom?! Where were we? It was clearly a dangerous situation.

We prayed.

As Amanda and I began to pray, we saw a man on a bicycle in the distance. He cycled towards us with a smile on his face and stopped to ask our driver what the problem was. The driver explained. The man smiled again. He pulled out a bag from the small basket on the front of his bike and took out the exact electrical part we needed and proceeded to fit it for us. Refusing any money, he happily cycled off and we were able to continue our journey.

It is only with hindsight that I wonder whether we met an angel that evening. What are the chances of a man cycling out of the middle of nowhere with the exact mystery electrical part that was needed for our model of car?

Another Angel?

God is so good at protecting us – better than any security guard. I don't go looking for trouble and am as careful as I can be about where we travel to and who is with us to ensure our safety. But I don't always get it right.

On one trip to Tanzania I walked out of the hotel grounds with my friend Charlotte Seymour. The two of us were a bit fed up with the 'over-protection' at the hotel and were keen to meet some of the real people outside of that environment.

We were fine at first, walking along the road and talking to some of the local people. We played football with some of the children, made up a little song with them and gently shared our faith with a few of the mums we met.

We began to walk into an area that seemed even more poverty stricken than most. As we did so, a man shouted to us. He was sitting in one of the small huts, working on a sewing machine. He said in perfect English:

'Ladies, I really wouldn't go beyond this point. There are some men down there. They have been drinking. Don't go any further.'

We took his advice and turned around. Speaking to some of the local pastors later, none of them knew of this man. They were not aware of anyone in that township that spoke any English, let alone with a perfect accent. Again, it is only as I look back on that episode that I wonder whether Charlotte and I met an angel. How come a man speaking perfect English was sat in a hut in the middle of nowhere?

Again, God was with us. We had known His blessing. And we had known His protection.

The Brothel

One of the things I've had to learn the hard way is that Jesus doesn't stand afar off; He doesn't sit aloof from mankind waiting for them to clean up their act before He'll intervene. I think sometimes the problem is that we want the world to clean up their act before we'll reach out with love – and then we wonder why the prostitutes and the drug addicts aren't walking through the doors of our church buildings. We need to be willing to reach into people's lives even when it's messy. Why? Because God reached into our mess. He reached into my world when I still stank of sin. The reality is that the drug addict's mess is visible for all to see, but it doesn't mean that our own mess is any less real simply because we learn to cover it over with good behaviour!

On a trip to Nigeria, I found myself speaking to a challenging audience. I had known well in advance that as a team we would be going to one of the brothels. I had prepared in advance by buying small silver necklaces for each of the women there, with a scripture attached to it: 'You are fearfully and wonderfully made' (see Psalm 139:14).

What I hadn't realised was that I would be speaking as well. At that time – one of our earlier missions – I didn't do a lot of speaking and was happy for others to take the lead. The two ladies leading in this situation were Toyin and Lorraine. Both were Nigerian, although Toyin lived in the UK.

It was Toyin who asked me to speak when we went to the brothel.

'Oh no, I don't really do that,' I said, 'I've got some things to give out but somebody else can speak – you can do it, Toyin!'

I was about to learn something about the determination of Nigerian women. Toyin looked at me with what I can only describe as fierceness, and said, 'Becky, I speak to the King in you, not the fool!'

I was shocked. I totally missed the compliment of her saying Jesus was in me and went straight to the 'fool' bit! Had I just been called a fool?

I recovered from the shock and went back to the hotel to prepare for the talk. As I prayed, I felt I heard God say that the women I would be speaking to cannot be bought at a price by any man – He had already paid the ultimate price. I had my talk.

When we got to the brothel it looked pretty much like any bar, except that adjoining the drinks area were numbers of doors into bedrooms.

The girls were all together to my left as I began to speak. But what I hadn't reckoned on were a lot of men standing to my right. I hadn't expected any men at all. What were they doing there? Then I realised. They were waiting for me to finish so they could 'get on with business'.

I was angry. Justice is my thing. I get so angry when I see injustice, and here it was right in front of me.

As I spoke, I remained wound up inside. I began, unconsciously at first, to turn more and more towards the girls and away from the men, until I had almost shut the men out of my vision. I spoke of God's love and mercy. Of His grace. Of His giving us the gift of life which we didn't deserve.

Then, as sure as anything I've ever heard from God, the Holy Spirit spoke to me. 'Didn't I die for them too?'

I was crushed. Even as I was speaking, I became so convicted by the shallowness of my attitude. I wanted the ground to swallow me up. I was such a hypocrite, so full of self-righteousness. In my head I had determined that the girls were worthy of salvation, but the men were not. I was speaking of mercy and grace at the same time as judging the whole room and determining who should go to hell and who should not. What right did I have to judge anyone?

At that moment, even as I was still speaking, I was looking into a metaphorical mirror. What I saw was my own heart – judgemental, critical, so full of my own self.

I chose in that moment. I chose to change my physical posture and speak to the whole room. But what I was really doing was changing my heart posture.

As I finished speaking and invited people to respond to the gospel, I saw a number of hands go up. All of the girls put up their hands. And as I looked to my right . . . a good number of the men.

A few minutes later as we were packing up to go, one of the men approached me.

'Madam, I need to tell you I'm a Muslim man. I don't believe in brothels. In fact I have never been in one before today. But as I walked past, I felt prompted to come inside, though I wasn't sure why. Now I know why. I need this Jesus.'

As we drove back to the hotel, tears began to flow.

'Lord, thank you for speaking to me. If You hadn't done that, all that man would have seen would have been a self-righteous English girl. Instead he saw You. Thank you. Thank you so much.'

Chapter Eight
The Field

As the plane touched down I knew this was different. As sure as anything, as I had been preparing for this trip, I had heard God speaking to me:

'Becky, now is the time. Look for land.'

It was hard not to smile all the time as we walked through customs control at Jomo Kenyatta International Airport, Nairobi. This was what I had been waiting for. This was back to the original call on my life. At long last I felt God was giving me the go-ahead. Numerous mission trips later, here it was – a start.

I had no real idea as to how it would happen, but as we drove out of the airport as a team and on our way to the first crusade in the city of Busia, I knew. I just knew.

We were going to meet Pastor Gerald Okoth and his wife Florence. It wasn't the first time. The first time had been on our honeymoon the year before.

I can remember being a little cross with Matt at the time. A lovely honeymoon in Mombasa – and here he was inviting a pastor to visit us!

Wedding Day

The wedding itself was a washout. It rained all day. As a result, there are only a few photos. But in other ways, it didn't matter at all. I was with my best friend and now my husband.

Nathan Morris had been the best man. Amanda Marrow was among the bridesmaids. Bishop Abu Koroma from Sierra Leone was the guest of honour and preached at the wedding. And the wedding venue? Father's House Church in Wath upon Dearne, Rotherham. Of course. Once a Rotherham girl, always a Rotherham girl.

Actually, rain on the wedding day is a sign of blessing in Africa, so maybe I can take that from the day.

As to Pastor Gerald and Florence visiting us on our honeymoon, I couldn't be cross for long. They are such a lovely couple and drove over sixteen hours to see us.

The Meeting

November 2009. The Blue York Hotel, Busia. The dining room. Pastor Gerald approaches. I'm so excited, I can hardly get my words out.

'Pastor, I have to tell you, I have to tell you! Do you remember when we met last year in Mombasa, I told you of God's call on my life?'

'Yes, Becky.'

'Well, what I didn't say was that part of that call was a clear word from God when I was eighteen years old. I heard God say I was going to build orphanages. I've been waiting for Him to show me more. And just before this trip, He did . . . He said, "Now is the time; look for land." Pastor, I wonder . . . do you know of any land? Are you aware of how we can begin to build?'

Pastor Gerald's response is a surprise to me.

He starts to cry.

'Becky, I've just been given a plot of land. I've just been given a field. It was sorted out yesterday. It's yours. You can have it.'

It was a remarkable response from a wonderful man of God. Someone who can be trusted and someone we have worked with for many years now.

Unbeknown to me, Gerald had had his own passion to start children's homes for many years, but his response to God at the time had been, 'How? I'm just a Kenyan guy.'

And here we were. From two parts of the world. Just a Kenyan guy meeting just a Rotherham girl. Joined together by a wonderful God who never forgets a calling and always answers a prayer.

Gerald arranged for me to be on one of the teams that would be visiting the village where the land was located.

Bumala B

Bumala B is a remote as it gets; it's the 'bush-bush' of Africa. The drive from Kisumu airport is stunning, as you watch African life unfold. I saw men sitting by the road smashing large rocks, breaking them up into smaller stones for building work. I watched as tiny children wandered around looking for old tyres to play with.

The mommas can be seen walking for miles with huge buckets of water on their heads, busy with that day's cleaning chores. The sugar factory we drive past in Mumias smells sickly; there's almost a metal taste in the air. The rubbish heaps are burning away, bringing with it their own smells.

But then, after ninety minutes of driving, we turn off the nicely laid tarmac road and onto the bumpy dirt tracks towards Bumala B. The village is stunning: rolling fields of maize with mud huts upon mud huts. Some of the huts have metal roofs whilst many still have the picture-perfect thatch roofs.

People are working in their *shambas* – their personal farms – tilling the land and collecting their maize or vegetables.

Kids line the dirt tracks walking back and forth to school. Motorbikes are whizzing past at full speed on the little mud tracks; they are the main form of transport in the village. The dirt tracks don't always widen enough for cars once you're in the thick of the village so walking on foot or travelling on a motorbike is the easiest way of getting around.

It's a strange name for a village. Bumala B. In the middle of nowhere. It's Gerald's home village. Not the biggest of places. But it has a church building. A tin shack really, with a floor made of cow dung. Fifty people at the morning service.

And after the meeting – the field.

There it was. Just next door. This was to be the answer. This was the fulfilment of a teenager's dream. This was God taking me on the next steps of the journey. And I was ready to embrace it.

It took time. It took persistence. And it took three years of hard work and fundraising. Three years of speaking to churches and charities. Three years in the midst of working with the Bay of the Holy Spirit revival and in seeing my beautiful Josiah born. Three years from seeing the field to the eventual opening.

Today we have a home for one hundred orphans on that land.

The Screams

The opening for the children's home was to be 12th December 2012 – 12.12.12. Memorable.

It was memorable for another reason as well. Let me take you there.

It's a week before we open the home in 2012. I'm staying in local accommodation, preparing for the big day. With me are my sister

Donna and my friend Lindsey Everatt. It's late in the evening and we've gone to bed, but I can hear Donna and Lindsey's conversation.

'Donna, can you feel it? Sort of a darkness? I don't like it.'

'Yes, I can feel it too.'

I shout to them from the next room. 'Just start worshipping. That will deal with it.'

And with that, I turn over to sleep.

A few seconds later there is a woman screaming. Not an ordinary scream. It is harrowing. I've not heard a scream like it. Then there's another scream. This time it's clearly a little girl's scream. This sounds serious – life threatening. I'm up in a moment.

'What was that?' I asked.

'I don't know, but I'm not sure we should go out,' says Donna.

Kevin, one of the local boys staying with us to protect us, comes through.

'Please don't go out – it's not safe. I've called the police.'

'But the police might take forever,' I say.

'They will come,' says Kevin. 'And besides, I'm supposed to keep you safe. Pastor Gerald will be very unhappy with me if you go out.'

By now I have my sweatshirt on over my pyjamas and I'm putting on my shoes.

'You're not going, Becky!' shouts Donna. 'You're going nowhere!'

'Yes I am. It could be a matter of life and death. How can we not respond?'

As I stand to go out, Donna comes behind me and, with no warning, wraps her arms around me in a vice-like grip. As a teaching assistant, she has learned some of the methods for disabling violent pupils and is trying them out on me.

Despite Donna not being as strong as me, (in my opinion as the feisty youngest sibling) I can't move and am shouting for her to let me go.

'No, Becky!' shouts Donna. 'How can I go back to Mum and Dad and tell them why you've not come home? You're not going out!'

In the end, all four of us decide to go. There are no street lamps and it's been raining. Within a few seconds, our pyjamas are soaked in mud.

The house is just a few doors down. It is owned by a young widow who manufactures a local alcoholic drink to help make ends meet. As a result of that, there are various men around her house most of the time, and a number of them were getting more than alcohol. One of them has got violent with the woman.

The police arrive and we are able to go back to bed.

The next day we go over again to the house. There are two young girls, aged eight and five, living with their mother. They are not well looked after and have to witness the men each night sleeping with their mother. It is clear that the mother is unable to care for the girls, so with some further discussions, we agree to take Christine and Valentine into the new home.

Full Circle

When Christine and Valentine first arrived, they were so fearful, especially of men. Gerald is the kindest of people and has a very gentle manner with the children, but they were even afraid of him and used to hide behind me, physically shaking if Gerald or any other man came into the room.

Over a period of time they have adjusted and today are the happiest of children.

It was only later that Gerald told me the rest of the story.

Just before our first arrival in Bumala B in 2009 to look at the land, Gerald had been caring for a man with cancer. He did all he could to care for him and paid a number of the hospital bills. Before the man died, and in recognition of all that Gerald had done to look after him, the man wanted to do something. He had no money. But he had a field.

The man with cancer was the one who gave the land for the orphanage. And that man with cancer was the father of Christine and Valentine. The blessing has come full circle.

As I looked out on the land that first day in November 2009, I had no idea of the story behind it, no idea of how God would bring blessing to the children of the man that had given the land. But I knew this was the land to build on. I knew this was the answer to my prayers. And I knew that God had been faithful.

Even Now

My story of the land is a miraculous one. One of God answering. But He did so at the right time. There was a lot of waiting. It would have been easy to see the dream die.

And so for each of us. Do you have dreams in God? Are there things God has spoken to you about that are yet to be fulfilled? Can I encourage you – hold on. It was hard for me as an eighteen-year-old, hearing the call of God on my life, knowing I would be developing children's homes, yet not seeing anything happen.

I tried – boy did I try! But I had to wait for God's timing. And His timing doesn't always fit with ours.

One of my favourite Bible stories concerns Martha. Her brother Lazarus died and Jesus didn't show up. When she hears Jesus is coming, she goes out to meet him. This is what the Bible says:

'So when Martha heard that Jesus was coming, she went and met him, but Mary remained seated in the house. Martha said to

Jesus, "Lord, if you had been here, my brother would not have died. But even now I know that whatever you ask from God, God will give you'" (John 11:20-22).

I love Martha's attitude. She is mourning the loss of her brother – he's been dead for four days now. But the cry on her lips is 'even now'! Martha shows real character at that point. She still believes. Despite the situation, she is holding on. Even now Jesus can intervene. And, of course, He does. Jesus raises Lazarus from the dead.

Martha's hope appeared to be dead. In fact, dead and buried! She cries out to Jesus, 'If you had just been here, my brother would not have died.' You can hear the heartbreak in her voice as she says it.

Maybe for you, as you read these words, there needs to be an 'even now' cry to the Lord. His timetable is not ours, but hold on, keep pressing in, keep asking. Cry out 'even now' over dreams that appear to have died and see what God will do. Cry out 'even now' over relationships that have failed, over loved ones away from God. Even in the midst of pain and disappointment, let's put the cry on our lips. Shout it out. 'Even now, Lord! Even now!'

Chapter Nine
Bay of the Holy Spirit

'But Cleddie, who is this Nathan Morris?'

'Believe me, John, you want him at your conference.'

The conversation, in the spring of 2010, was between Pastor Cleddie Keith and Pastor John Kilpatrick.

John had been greatly used in heading up the revival at Brownsville, Pensacola. Cleddie is a good friend of ours. He had been over to the UK and had visited Wath church. In his words, 'I've turned over a stone and all these radicals have run out.' Such was the impact we were having through Nathan's ministry at the Wath meetings.

On Pastor Cleddie's recommendation, John Kilpatrick invited Nathan to speak at the conference for the final two days. Because of my own experience at Brownsville, I was delighted to be asked by Nathan to join him and Matt in the meetings. They were held at the Church of His Presence in Mobile, Alabama. The conference itself was called The Open Heavens Conference. And so it turned out to be.

Although delighted to be there, I had one eye on the exit door. Matt and I had arranged for some further preaching together with a short holiday on the island of Hawaii after the conference. We'd not had a real holiday in a long time, and the thought of a few days' rest on the beautiful sands of these tropical islands was rather appealing.

We never got there.

The Revival

The presence of the Holy Spirit at the meetings was tangible. Many were getting healed. There were significant miracles in the meetings and, to Pastor John's delight, they were among folk he knew – people from his local church. Friends who he knew would not be inclined to exaggerate what was happening to them. Such were the healings and the miracles it felt like there was a particular Holy Spirit presence. It felt like God wanted to bless us in a special way. And that is exactly what God did. God was with us, there to bless us. The worship was electric. The power of the Holy Spirit was such that on occasion it was hard to even stand in the meetings.

As the final day approached, Pastor John spoke to Nathan.

'This reminds me so much of Father's Day 1995. You can't go. You must stay!'

The reference John was making was to the start of the Holy Spirit moving powerfully in Brownsville, Pensacola. The comment from John was made with an awareness of what had happened on that occasion, and we therefore took his words seriously.

We continued the meetings each night from then on, well beyond the original conference dates.

Delia Knox, a well-known gospel singer, attended the meetings. She had been knocked down nearly twenty-three years earlier by a drunk driver and had been wheelchair bound since then. Delia was one of the miracles. She walked.

This got the attention of not just the local news but national news. Fox News TV channel arrived to film the meetings. ABC News featured Delia's miracle in a *Nightline* report as part of its *Faith Matters* series. The *Daily Mail* newspaper in the UK ran her story. Channel 7 *Eyewitness News* covered the story as well, including Delia meeting her parents for the first time since being able to walk. All this took the coverage of the revival to another level. God TV began to broadcast it every single night. It became known worldwide as the Bay of the Holy Spirit Revival. This is a reference to the original Spanish name for Mobile Bay, right next to where we were holding the meetings.

After two weeks, I had to return home. I was a full-time nurse at that time and was back on my shifts. I was desperate to give up my job and get back out to the revival – especially as I had left Matt behind, which was our first significant time apart since marriage.

We knew it would be best for me to continue to work at the hospital at least in the short term. It was a hard time for me. I missed Matt. I even got to smelling his clothes in the wardrobe, I was missing him so much!

Alabama

The original meetings had started in July 2010. By September they were still going every night, with no end in sight. God was continuing to bless. Miracles were continuing to happen. It was in August that Matt and I made the decision to relocate to Alabama, at least in the short to medium term. I quit my job and in September found myself living in a small house in Daphne, Alabama, owned by someone in the church who kindly allowed us to live there. Likewise, we were given a car. It was owned by a man in the church who had a car dealership and he generously allowed us to use it for free, with us just paying for fuel.

I became part of the worship team and worked on the staff team for Pastor John's church as well as being responsible for all the recordings of the testimonies from the revival. This included getting proof where I could for the miracles. We have files full of CT scans and doctors' reports confirming incredible miracles. I carried one around with me for a while, it was so astonishing. Caleb was a young boy and the scans showed the before and after prayer pictures of his brain. One with a large tumour. One completely clear.

Despite the joy of all God was doing and my front-row seat in the revival in terms of ministry, I was still tense. The tenseness came from a field we owned in Africa. I felt God asking me to lay down the vision for a while – but I must admit, I kept picking it up again!

'Oh God, when will it happen? When can we start work in Kenya? How will it happen, Lord?'

My prayers were both consistent and rather regular on this issue!

Overseas Rebecca

It had been a long week already. I was tired. Rather than be at the front of the meeting on that Thursday evening, I crept in at the back. It was no good though – I was too well known and within a minute there were people wanting to talk to me. I have no problem with that usually, but on this occasion I just wanted time on my own.

I decided to leave the civic centre we were meeting in and go for a walk. The building is right on the bay so there are some lovely views over the water.

After a while I went back in again, but no sooner had I done so than I felt as clear as anything, the Holy Spirit telling me to return outside! I obeyed. And there, across the bay, was a sight that would stay with me.

The bay has a lot of tankers and cargo ships and as I went out one of them was passing by. I looked at the name on the side of the ship. *Overseas Rebecca.*

Wow. There it was. Was this to do with the children's home? Was that what God was saying? I called my friend Charlotte outside to look with me, and to take a photo. We were too late with the photo, though, because as soon as the ship cleared the bay and was out into the deeper waters, it sped up.

'Well, Becky, I could be wrong but I think this is to do with the children's home in Kenya.'

Charlotte said it before I could articulate it myself. As I walked back in to the meeting, my mind was in overdrive. I walked right to the front of the meeting and lay on the floor near to the altar area we used to call people forward in response to the preaching. I knew I'd be left alone there – and I needed to have time with God.

As soon as I lay down, I heard God speaking to me inwardly.

'Becky, just like the ship sped up when it got into the deep, that's what I'm going to do with OneByOne. As you go out in faith into deeper waters, I'm going to speed up all that is happening.'

Changes

I knew from God's prompt that night and the amazing name on the ship that there were going to be changes. In fact there were two very big changes in our lives.

Matt and I had been trying for a baby. When we went out to Alabama, we decided to stop trying for a while just because of the different environment. The moment we stopped trying was the moment I fell pregnant.

And I had a name.

I had told Matt as soon as we were engaged that the name of our boy, if it was a boy, would be Josiah. I had read the story of the young king Josiah when I was a little girl and it had stuck with me. I knew that any baby boy born would be called Josiah. It was difficult to have the conversation with Matt though.

'Matt, I know that you will be head of the home. And I know that we will need to share in all the big decisions in life. But I also need to tell you that if you marry me and we have a baby boy, he will be called Josiah. I'm not giving you a choice. You can name any other children; we can make joint decisions on everything, but not on this!'

Bless him, Matt was more than happy to go along with my rather determined approach.

Being pregnant just after arriving in Alabama was not ideal. But we coped and were back home in Rotherham in the later stages of the pregnancy.

That was when the second big change came.

Nathan called around one night to talk.

'Becky, I need to let you go.'

'What do you mean, Nathan?'

'I need to let OneByOne have its own identity separate from Shake the Nations.'

'Nathan, are you just saying that because I'm eight months' pregnant and you can't work with me anymore?'

'No, honestly, Becky, that's not it. I really do feel God is saying it. I think there is more for you as you step out in faith.'

Nathan was very generous with a seed payment towards OneByOne but, perhaps because of my hormones in this later stage of pregnancy, I was not happy! It felt like I was being sacked! By one of my best friends no less. Nathan had been best man at our wedding and Matt had been best man for Nathan and Rachel. We were close. We were family. And it felt like a family member had just walked out.

It was hormones, of course. Or maybe it was mixed with emotions. It meant I had to set up our charity on its own. It meant I had to fundraise directly. And it meant I had to trust God even more.

Even If Not

With hindsight I can see Nathan was right, but at the time I found it so hard. I felt abandoned and unable to move forward. It was a challenging time. Would God be with me on the new venture? Would we survive without the backing of Shake the Nations? Were the dreams going to die?

Three of my favourite Old Testament characters are Shadrach, Meschach and Abednego. You probably know the story. The three men were instructed to fall down and worship the golden image that King Nebuchadnezzar had constructed. They would not. The penalty for not obeying the king was a fiery furnace.

The response of the three men to the king's threat is instructive.

'Our God whom we serve is able to deliver us from the burning fiery furnace, and he will deliver us out of your hand, O king. But if not, be it known to you, O king, that we will not serve your gods or worship the golden image that you have set up' (Daniel 3:17-18).

Shadrach, Meschach and Abednego declared to the king that God was able to rescue them from the fiery furnace (and He did!) but they go on to say that 'even if not', they will still not worship the image the king has made.

Sometimes we have to make our stand on the 'even if not'. We trust God. But even if he doesn't answer – or answer in the way we expect – we are still not going to compromise!

There may be disappointments in life. There will certainly be circumstances that we don't understand. But we deal with the disappointments and we continue to look to God. Even if not . . . He's still our God.

With the move away from Shake the Nations, it meant declaring along with Shadrach, Meschach and Abednego that the God whom we serve would deliver us. It meant taking risks. It meant 'Overseas Rebecca', it meant trusting that God was going to do what God had promised to do.

We were going out into deep waters and the speed of everything was about to increase.

Chapter Ten
The Year Before the Beginning

July 8th 2011. Matt and I are travelling up the motorway to meet Ken and Lois Gott. They lead the Bethshan group of churches in the north-east of England and were greatly used by God in what became known as the Sunderland Renewal. I was still grieving about our break from Nathan's ministry and Ken and Lois had been a great help and comfort to me during this time.

The reason I remember the date so clearly, though, is because of what happened as we got out of the car at the service station. My waters broke. Josiah was on the way.

I remember Matt and Ken asking if we could still have our coffee first, but I was adamant. The baby was on the way. That evening at Rotherham hospital, a beautiful 7lb 4oz baby boy was born. His name, of course, was Josiah!

I had left Matt to decide on the middle name. He pondered this over a couple of months, researching various names. But as he registered the birth, he still wasn't sure. Nor was I sure what I would read on the birth certificate. As I looked at the document, I read the name 'Josiah Matthew'. For all that pondering and researching, Matt had given him his own name!

Problems

Things weren't going to plan at the hospital. No matter how hard I tried, Josiah wouldn't feed. The nurses assured me that he would and that as a first-time mum I was just finding things a bit difficult to start with.

At first I accepted their advice but as the hours went on, things got no better. Josiah was still not feeding. After nearly two days, Josiah had stopped even crying for a feed and had become quite lethargic. As a paediatric nurse I knew something was wrong, despite the midwife assuring me Josiah was just being a bit slow to start feeding. As for Matt, he was concerned that I was becoming a psychotic woman full of hormones, because everyone was assuring him that the baby was fine.

Eventually, on the fourth day a different midwife came on duty. This was someone I knew from my own work as a nurse, and thankfully she paid attention. The consultant was called and Josiah was moved to the special unit in order to be fed via a tube. I relaxed. But not for long.

Coming back onto the ward, the first thing I noticed was that Josiah had now been put onto a drip. This was not a normal way to feed a baby that was not feeding naturally.

I asked the nurse what was happening. The look on her face as she asked me whether the doctor had seen me caused me to panic. I knew from my own experience as a nurse that if the problem was a small one, the nurse would be quite open about it. But if it was a bigger problem, a nurse would generally defer to a doctor. And this was what this nurse was doing.

The doctor sat me down.

'Becky, Josiah has vomited up everything we have been trying to feed him. He's growing weak and we don't know what the problem is. We are going to put him on a ventilator and send him to Sheffield Children's Hospital.'

I cried.

Operation

The news at Sheffield Children's Hospital was no better. The surgeon explained that normally he would not operate on a baby like Josiah because he was too weak.

'Normally, Mrs Murray, I would wait until we had got some food into Josiah so he was strong enough to deal with the anaesthetic. But . . .'

I held my breath.

'If I delay I don't think he will make it. It's a risk operating on a weak baby like this, but I don't think we have a choice.'

My whole world was collapsing. This was my promised baby boy. My Josiah. The name I felt God had given me as a little girl. Was He about to take my baby away?

Matt and I clung to each other and to God over the next few hours. When I was a mess, Matt was strong for me. When he was going through it, I found strength to keep going. We learned a lot about the value of a good marriage in those hours.

After a sleepless night and with tears rolling down my face, the surgeon came into the room.

'He's made it. He's come through the operation. We know what the problem is and we can help him through.'

By now I was sobbing, holding on to Matt.

'Thank you, Jesus,' I whispered through the tears.

Josiah had Hirschsprung's disease – a birth defect in which nerves are missing from parts of the intestine. It means he can't digest food properly.

He stayed on a ventilator for two weeks and, after being allowed home, we had to take him back for five further operations in that first year of his life.

The Year from Hell

I know it wasn't but it felt like it. 2011 felt like the year from hell. My own hormones were all over the place with the birth of Josiah. His illness was a constant concern. I was stressed because we were no longer part of Shake the Nations. And there was still a field in Kenya without a children's home and without finance.

All this placed a considerable strain on a marriage that was still in its early years. There were times when Matt and I were not coping during that year. Times when it seemed that everything was closing in.

What was God doing? I felt I had lost my identity. I couldn't identify as a mum – I felt a failure in not being able to help my baby. I couldn't identify as a wife and felt our marriage was failing. I couldn't identify with my ministry – here, too, I seemed to be failing with no support coming through and a new charity to establish. And even my singing was failing me. Until then I'd been part of worship teams wherever we went but, with Josiah's birth, I lost my singing voice. I have no idea why, but I could no longer sing well enough to sing solo or even be in a choir.

All this was playing on my mind. As I look back now, I see it was the year before the beginning and not the year from hell. It was the year before OneByOne began to grow and prosper. The year before God began to work financial miracles.

Valleys

It was a year of testing. Sure, there was an enemy keen for us to fail. But God sometimes allows tests in our lives. It leads us to Him. Even in the deepest valleys we need not fear.

I've mentioned this passage already, but there's a particular story of a valley in Ezekiel 37 that resonates with me:

'The hand of the LORD was upon me, and he brought me out in the Spirit of the LORD and set me down in the middle of the valley; it was full of bones. And he led me around among them, and behold, there were very many on the surface of the valley, and behold, they were very dry. And He said to me, "Son of man, can these bones live?" And I answered, "O Lord GOD, you know."'

God will sometimes take us on a journey just as He did with Ezekiel. He took him on a walk through a valley; he didn't run quickly through the valley, neither did they stand at a distance looking on. The Bible says God led him back and forth among the dry bones.

The verses connected for me. This was what God had been doing. It seemed to have been a whole year of dry bones – with me walking back and forth among them! Hard as it seemed, though, I couldn't stand back and watch; nor could I run through the problems quickly.

Then suddenly, God turns and ask Ezekiel a question – can these bones live? Ezekiel's probably thinking, 'Why on earth is He asking me? He's God and I'm not. Only You know, God.'

God speaks to Ezekiel again:

'Then he said to me, "Prophesy over these bones, and say to them, O dry bones, hear the word of the LORD. Thus says the

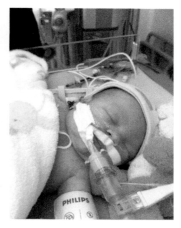

Felicity

Becky with Felicity, Amanda Marrow and Solomon. Felicity was the catalyst for OneByOne in my heart. She presumed my 50p gift purchased her body as she was so used to being abused as a street kid. This moment in 2006 turned my exciting promise into a non-negotiable lifestyle. I had to give my life for this – even if it would only ever help one child.

Josiah in 2011 – he had to have five major surgeries within his first year of life. Thankfully now he is healthy and well.

Original 42

On 12/12/12 we opened the King's children's home in Kenya with 42 children.

Homebase programme launched 2013

We had children desperate to move into our children's home, despite them having families. This was due to the extreme poverty in our village, so we launched the Homebase programme, accepting the poorest children living within a 5km radius of our home. We educate and feed these children daily but then they return back to their own homes and families every evening. Wherever possible we keep families together, but this programme enables every child to have hope for the future.

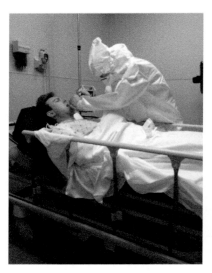

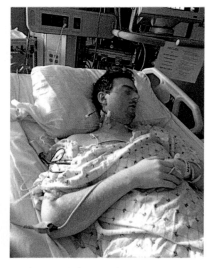

Matthew in Isolation

In October 2014 Matthew was diagnosed with Malaria but also quarantined with suspected Ebola. Thankfully he didn't have Ebola, but the Malaria almost cost him his life.

Matthew given hours to live

The Malaria began to attack his major organs, his heart, lungs, liver and kidneys were all in organ failure and he was given 3 hours left to live. This is one of the most incredible healings I have ever had the joy of witnessing! To this day I meet strangers who tell me they saw the social media post asking for help and they prayed for Matthew. To everyone who prayed, thank you!

Renew Church

In January 2015, just 3 months after Matthew had been given 3 hours left to live, we became the senior pastors of Renew Church in Uttoxeter, Staffordshire. Both the town and the people quickly became home for us!

Sri Lanka

In 2015 God laid the nation of Sri Lanka on our hearts, with a passion to help the war widows. For the first two years we ran a feeding programme to help feed the ladies and their children every day.

Sri Lanka

As many of our war widows were young ladies, we decided to help them establish their own micro businesses through sewing centres. OneByOne now runs 7 sewing centres across the north of Sri Lanka.

Dignity Project

We launched the Dignity Project in Kenya in September 2015 after several children had gone missing in our village.

Dignity Project

We were shocked to see how this initiative took off around the world. To date we have reached over 17,000 girls across Kenya, Pakistan, Sierra Leone, Brazil, India and South Africa. We are now starting in Uganda, Zambia and Zimbabwe.

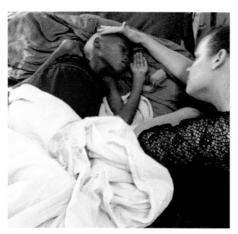

Brenda

This is little Brenda, she tragically died just a few days after this photo was taken, but because of her, her village of Mauko is now being transformed. A village that was renown for gang-rape, murder and witchcraft, now has a thriving church and since the church was planted there hasn't been one murder up until today!

Brick Factories

After taking the Dignity Project into Pakistan in 2018 we discovered thousands of slaves in Brick Factories. We knew we had to do something to help these children trapped in slavery.

King's Pakistan

In May 2019 we opened our second King's children's home, this time in Pakistan rescuing 52 children out of slavery.

Slaves become children

Our kids had only ever known how to be slaves, with some of them working 14 hour days. Now they can be children. We have also launched Sunday school in several of the brick factories so that we can bring hope and life to children whom the brick masters won't yet release.

Kenya continues to grow

Our home in Kenya continues to grow, we currently have over 200 children in our care. We have also launched Sunday school in almost 20 schools across our village and sub-county and so now reach over 10,000 children every week.

Josiah on the mission

As a family there's nothing we love more than to be all together on the field. Josiah has joined us on several missions trips across Kenya and South Africa.

My role models

My kids inspire me constantly. They have overcome so much abuse and hardship and yet radiate the joy and love of Jesus in a way that both captivates and challenges me daily.

Giant family

I could not be more thankful for our giant international family.

Open doors

God continually surprises me with the doors He keeps opening. Over the last couple of years TBN and other TV and radio networks have opened up asking to share the stories of what God is doing through OneByOne. My hearts prayer is that through it, many other people will be inspired to lay their lives down for the gospel too and that as we do we can truly reach the world OneByOne!

Lord GOD to these bones: Behold, I will cause breath to enter you, and you shall live.'"

God turns the solution to the problem back into the hands of Ezekiel, saying, 'You prophesy! You speak life where there is currently only death. You speak hope where there is currently only hopelessness; you declare victory where there is currently only defeat!'

Just as God worked with Ezekiel, so too He works with us.

The miracle was in Ezekiel's mouth.

So often in crisis moments we look to God, waiting for this great 'come through' moment, but God wanted the victory to come through Ezekiel. Yes, they were God's words, it was God's breath, it was God attaching the tendons and adding the flesh, but He didn't want to do that without Ezekiel. He wanted His words and His breath to flow through Ezekiel.

Likewise the miracle is in our mouth today! God longs to do a miracle in our impossible situations but He wants to do it in and through us. He doesn't want to do it without our mouth, without our hands, without our heart.

He wants you to speak into being that which you can't even see yet. To speak into being that which you can't even comprehend with your mind.

If you want dry things to live, then open your mouth! God can make the driest of situations in your life come alive. But He needs you to be involved in the process.

Maybe your dry bones are a business; maybe it's a marriage; maybe it's the health of a loved one. No matter what you see in your circumstances you have a choice. You can either see only death, or you can see possibilities.

For me, I had to make a choice. Through the tears and heartache of that year, I chose to see possibilities again. I chose to see a God who could heal my baby; a God who would answer my prayers.

It wasn't easy, and as I write these words I appreciate that many reading them will find it as hard as I did. But in the end we have to ask a question.

What are we going to do with the dry bones in our life?

Chapter Eleven
Bananas

It started with a conversation in Starbucks. Pastor Cleddie Keith was visiting.

'Becky, I've got a prophetic word for you.'

I sat up and paid attention.

He wasn't joking. It was a prophetic 'word'. The word was 'bananas'. That was it. He felt that somehow we would know what God was saying when it happened.

To be honest, if it had been anyone else I probably would have laughed it off. But this was our good friend Cleddie and he had a great track record with prophetic words.

I pondered the word for a while. Maybe, I thought, it would be a ship load of bananas for our Kenya initiative? Maybe that would open up some further connections? It seemed to me that everywhere I looked I was seeing advertisements for bananas after that! But nothing that made much sense.

It was almost two years later, at the start of 2012, that the word at long last made sense. And in a pretty amazing way.

The Sponsored Walk

Having established OneByOne as a separate charity, Matt and I were working hard to gain the finance we needed to get the building started in Kenya. With this in mind we visited Pastor Cleddie's church in Florence, Kentucky.

It was a good time. Matt preached and we raised some finance for the children's home as well as establishing some good relationships.

A young lady came up to me at the end of one of the services to let me know that she intended to organise a sponsored walk for OneByOne. I thanked her for her willingness to do this but, to be honest, I thought no more about it. How much money would a sponsored walk bring in, I thought. I'm from Rotherham and back home it would probably be around £50. That's the kind of figure I had in mind, anyhow.

It was a couple of weeks later that we received an email from the young lady to let us know that she had raised $19,000. That was some sponsored walk! I asked her how she had managed to gain so much in sponsorship. She explained that her family and friends had been incredibly generous, and between them she had raised around $4,000. The other $15,000 had come from just one person.

Matt asked the young lady whether there was a possibility, the next time we were out in Florence, of meeting the generous sponsor. She explained that this person wasn't keen on meeting people but that she would ask. To the surprise of the young lady, the individual agreed to meet us.

A Cup of Tea

A few months later, we are out with Pastor Cleddie again and we arrange with the young lady to go out and meet the kind person who had been so generous with the sponsorship. His house is an hour or so away from Cleddie's and, as we are driving out, I begin to notice a change in the surroundings. The houses are definitely getting bigger and bigger.

At one point we pass the house that the astronaut Neil Armstrong used to live in, and soon after we arrive at our destination. It's down a long drive and as we pull up I see how large the house actually is. We are greeted by an older gentleman, by then in his late eighties. He is very unassuming and invites us in. We meet his wife and the two of them invite us to sit down.

I had assumed I was there to say 'thank you' for the gift, but as the conversation gets underway it begins to resemble more of a job interview. The questions about our charity are wide ranging and thorough. Matt and I answer as best we can. I am still thinking at this stage that I am simply thanking them for the gift and that they are just being thorough in ensuring they have sponsored something worthwhile.

I am wrong.

At the end of the conversation, the cheque book is produced and they give me a cheque for a further $10,000. And I thought we were there for a cup of tea!

The gifts are by far the highest individual gifts we have received up until that point in time.

Matt is particularly intrigued. As we are leaving Matt says, 'Can I ask . . . Who are you?'

The gentleman gives his name. He explains that he was the owner of a gas station, that he had an ice cream company and had also been the owner at one time of the Cincinnati Reds baseball team.

'But,' he says, 'we actually made most of our fortune with another enterprise. We used to own Chiquita Bananas.'

Wow. There it is. Cleddie's prophetic 'word'. The continuing gifts from this kind couple over that year were the final payments for our children's home. Many others gave, mostly smaller amounts. And we are so grateful for every one.

Generosity

That same year we opened the children's home, in December 2012. Without a single penny owing.

People had given so generously. Our generous benefactor went on to give close to £100,000. In addition, there was another businessman who blessed us financially. He had been keen to see us off at the airport at the end of one trip. As we left, he put a cheque for $45,000 into our hands with the comment to Matt, 'That's for you, son. Go and rescue some more children and be blessed.'

All £150,000 for the home had come in on time; all the bills were paid. From the time we got the land until the opening, there was hardly a week went by without a payment being made to the bank, a cheque received in the post, a church making a donation, complete strangers offering to sponsor a child. God fulfils His promises.

As Matt and I have gone on to new ventures within our charity, we have found that God is always faithful in paying the bills. We pray 'give us this day our daily bread'. And it is 'this day'. He always provides on time. He's never late. But He never seems to be early either. I'd love Him to give me a millionaire or two so that I don't have to be overly concerned about the monthly bills, but God doesn't seem to work that way.

I remember the day we got the initial architect's bill for the design for the King's Children's Home. I remember holding the bill in my hands. I remember a moment of fear. All I had in the bank at the time was £1,000 – and that £1,000 had taken me months to raise. At that moment, the bill may as well have been for millions of pounds. I simply didn't have the money.

The enemy so often says to us, 'Did God say?' That was the first challenge in the Bible. He challenges our faith with lies.

I made a decision that day. I would give Him my £1,000. I would give Him all that I had.

And, of course, He was faithful with the rest.

Lack or Excess?

How do we give? When I gave that £1,000 it was all I had. But too often I only give from my excess. There is no sacrificial giving from excess.

I remember one time I was travelling back to the UK from Bumala B. I was late with my packing, so Jess, one of the girls in the home, was helping me.

She cut up some mangoes for me to eat on the journey. I encouraged her to keep one back for herself, but she insisted that I would need them. She assured me that she would be fed later.

It was only when I got to the airport I realised that I still had a lot of the mango left uneaten, so I gave it to Amos, my driver.

Jess had given from her lack. She hardly ever got to eat mangoes. Although common in Kenya, they are hard to get where we are in Bumala B. But when I got to the airport, I had no real use for what was left – I was giving from my excess.

It's a common picture in the Bible. We read of the widow giving everything she had left to Elijah for a meal (1 Kings 17). She only had a bit of flour and oil and was planning a last meal for her and her son before they died. The result of her obedience was miraculous food every day for the woman and her son.

She was obedient. She had no great revelation from God that she should do this thing. She simply obeyed Elijah. She had no guarantee as to what would happen next.

Let's give all we have. Let's meet the needs of others first, as this woman met Elijah's need. Let's give whatever is in our hands – and see how God blesses back in abundance.

Holding the Blue Container

I'm still learning of course.

There are many times when I cry out to God for finances. There are many days when it seems we don't have enough. But I always remember the blue container Amanda and I carried in Sierra Leone with the rice for the poor and how that container never ran out. How at the end, there seemed to be even more left than we started with. And I thank God for His faithfulness.

I metaphorically hold that blue container before God in prayer on numerous occasions. It's not always an easy financial journey, this giving and receiving, but it is a journey to embrace, and one that shows God to be faithful.

It's a journey of watershed moments – when I seemingly have had a choice as to whether to go forward or step back. I remember the 'warning words' about the bullets on that same trip to Sierra Leone. If Amanda and I had heeded them, would we ever have seen God's miraculous multiplication? Would I ever have seen later financial miracles? I'm grateful for the Holy Spirit boldness to step into all God has for us.

Chapter Twelve
Mother Bumala

The breeze is welcome, soothing, sweet. I push back the hair from my face and look out on the gathering, preparing to speak in Swahili and my best Luhya, the local tribal language in this area.

There are certain sounds and smells that always remind me I'm back home in Africa. As I stood there that afternoon, the stunning bird noises were almost at full volume. And there's always the choir that is the bugs, from crickets to the cicadas. The smells are as varied as the sounds, from rubbish being burned to the beautiful scents from the lilies and the wild orchids.

I look around. I hear them before I see them, the sound of kids running and giggling and shouting as they arrive for the opening.

There's my friend Lindsey, on the front row with the biggest of smiles on her face. Next to her are some good friends who have flown out to hold a gospel crusade on the adjacent land as part of our celebrations.

To the left I can see Christine and Valentine looking on from the edge of the crowd, our latest rescued children and, as I was to find out later, the children of the man who had donated the land before his death. Christine and Valentine stand just a little way off from forty other boys and girls – our first intake into the home.

To the right are the team that have just flown out from England, including Nick Jones, a professional videographer, who is kindly recording the event for us.

By my side stands Matt, beaming at me, encouraging me to hold it together as I speak.

On my other side is Gerald, the pastor who gave me the land, my fellow trustee and the person who will be overseeing the children's home on a daily basis. I notice a tear in his eye. This day is significant for him as much as for me. God had spoken to him years ago about starting a children's home but his response at the time was to question it, simply not knowing how it could happen.

But it did happen. And here we were – on 12th December 2012. The start of the Bumala B King's Children's Home.

The Evening Before

It nearly didn't happen.

As I sat down to eat on the evening before the opening, I casually asked Gerald how his meetings had gone that day. I was only asking out of politeness, thinking that the meetings had been to do with his work as an accountant. They hadn't been. They were to do with the opening of the home.

'Sister Becky, actually it's really bad news.'

'What do you mean?'

'I met with the planning officials today. They say we can't open tomorrow.'

'WHAT?!'

It's fair to say that at that point I wasn't taking this news very calmly!

'Yes, they say that until there has been a final inspection of the building, the children can't move in.'

I was so angry. We had planned to open the previous Easter but had been delayed by bureaucracy at the time. To be told the night before that we weren't allowed to open was simply unacceptable. I knew that we had jumped through every administrative hoop imaginable to get this far and had had numerous meetings with pretty much anyone and everyone linked to giving permission for the home to open.

I knew too that there had been a rumour going around the villages that I was a white witch. It's hard to stop rumours at the best of times and there was no way we could stop this one. The villages have no other form of news. There are no newspapers and there is no television, so everything is by word of mouth. Sadly, the gossip this produced about me was not helpful when dealing with the authorities.

I slammed my hand down on the table.

'Gerald, that home is opening tomorrow. I'm not having this! They have had every opportunity for a final inspection. They simply can't say on the day before we open that it's not going ahead. Get me the official on the phone now!'

'Sister Becky, can I suggest we calm down a bit and pray?'

'It's not praying we need right now, Gerald, it's action!'

I was marching up and down by now. Everything had been arranged. People had flown in for the event. The children had been living in friends' houses for too long and needed to move in officially.

Gerald managed to get his brother and a local pastor to come over and pray with us. Donna, my sister, had gone back home by this time, but my friend Lindsey was still with us. In fact, it was so late in the evening that Lindsey had already gone to bed. But when she heard all the praying and crying out to God, she came and joined us, still wearing her pyjamas.

We made a decision at the end of that prayer time. The next morning, Gerald called the planning office and spoke to one of the supervisors. We didn't give them a choice. We said to them that we were going ahead with the opening and that the building inspector could come at any time as we were ready for the inspection. Thankfully this was accepted. And I'm glad it was as the inspector didn't actually show up until the following February!

We had a lot to do the next morning in preparation for the ceremony. As the team prepared a small platform and organised the food, the children ran around excitedly. One of the boys waving at me was Emmanuel.

Emmanuel

If ever there was a reason for starting the home, there it was in front of me. Emmanuel's older sister had died and his father turned to alcohol. It led to his father fighting with his mother. One night the arguments were so violent, Emmanuel hid in a cupboard. When he eventually came out, his mother was so angry with him for hiding that she struck him with a machete. You can still see the scar on the top of his head.

Emmanuel and his brother Seth were not well looked after. When their father died by drowning, things got worse. Their mother refused to let them leave the house and they were required to carry out household tasks in horrendous conditions. Emmanuel and his brother were increasingly neglected and, when we found them, they were close to death with their mother having walked out.

Shaddy

As I began to lay out the ceremony bunting, Shadrach – Shaddy to me – came to say hello. He and his younger brother Bernard had been rescued from a tragic situation. When a social worker first found them, all we could ascertain was that their father had died and then a couple of years later their mum had died. It took a while longer to piece together what had actually happened.

It turned out that his father, at the time he died, had three wives. All three continued to live together after his death, but two of the wives decided to murder the third wife in order to have more land between them. That third wife was the mother to Shaddy and Bernard.

The two women stoned her to death. In front of Shaddy. They then continued to look after Shaddy and Bernard as if nothing had happened. In other words, the brothers were being cared for by the two murderers of their mother.

Even then, we didn't get to the end of the story. It took Shaddy longer still to open up to us about his older brother. We had been aware that the two boys had an older brother, but we had assumed he was a lot older and away from home. This turned out not to be the case. It was when I asked Shaddy just in conversation one day how his older brother was, that the truth came out.

When I asked the question, Shaddy began to cry. This in itself was unusual as the culture in the tribe is that teenage boys never cry. But here he was in floods of tears. So much so, he couldn't even speak and had to come back to see me later and tell me the story.

When the boy's mother had been murdered, the older brother, Vincent, became the main carer, shielding them to an extent from the two wives who had killed their mother. In order to help survive, Vincent reared a few chickens. But the problem was, these chickens kept disappearing. Vincent decided to stay up one night to try and catch whoever was stealing them.

Sure enough, someone arrived to take yet another of the chickens. The boy shone his torch on the man, only to find it was one of his uncles. Vincent confronted the uncle and accused him of stealing all the chickens. There was a problem with this. In the local culture, it was disrespectful to ever challenge an older person, even if they were wrong. The uncle was so shamed by what had happened, he picked up a machete and began to attack the boy. He cut him on the neck, but thankfully it missed the main artery.

As a result of this attack, the uncle was put in jail. Shaddy hoped this would be the end of it and he and Bernard could then continue to live with their older brother in peace.

The day came when the uncle was released from jail. Sadly, his one thought was to avenge his accuser. That same night, the uncle came to the hut where the three boys were sleeping together and strangled Vincent to death.

Shaddy had witnessed both his mother's murder and now his older brother's murder. It seems his younger brother Bernard was too young to really know what was going on, but inevitably it strongly affected Shaddy.

It has taken time, but Shaddy has begun to change. Although he struggles academically, he's very creative with what he can make with his hands. He's a good runner and is eager to enter competitions. He has always been quiet and withdrawn but, with our help and friendship, he has changed. He is still traumatised by what has happened but we see the change too. We see the smile. We see the trust. We see the hope.

The Ceremony

The time came for the ceremony and the opening of the home. Ceremonies in Kenya last a long time. After I had spoken, many others wanted to speak as well. But eventually, as we reached the end of a long afternoon of speeches, I stood once more and, in Swahili, I spoke to the children. With tears in my eyes, I said 'Karibu nyumbani: welcome home.'

Forty-two children entered the home that day. There were meant to be more but because the rumours of me being a white witch were circulating, including that I was going to curse the children and they would die, relatives of the orphaned children had stopped them from coming. We overcame this through time and today we have one hundred children in the home, which is the maximum it will take.

During the next few days I worked with our two newly appointed house mothers to settle the children. Needless to say, that first night none of them slept – they were far too excited! On the Sunday following, I spoke in the church Sunday school with all the children attending. I was so excited when many of them gave their lives to Christ. Later the same week we had the thrill of baptising some of the older children.

They Are All My Favourites

All the children are my favourites, but the original forty-two in my first OneByOne home are particularly special. As I stood in front of them on the day we travelled back home, there were tears in my eyes.

Emmanuel and Shadrach were chasing each other around the car. There was Meshach, walking towards me; he's always climbing trees. I could give him a new jumper every morning and it would be torn the same day.

Standing next to Meshach was Ivene. She's the cheeky one with such an adorable charm. When she first discovered sunglasses she went around collecting them from the team and prancing around wearing them. She has such a combination of boldness and charm. My team fall for it every time!

As the children gathered around me to say goodbye, I saw Nellie. One of the smallest and shyest of the children, but when she thinks no one is watching her she quietly twirls around. Her favourite item is a princess dress we brought out with us. She is forever wearing it – and forever twirling around in it!

Joan was quietly standing by the car. Her parents and all her siblings had died of HIV. Joan also has HIV and has little energy, often falling asleep in school. Mohammed was with her this morning. His dad had died and his mum is blind. Mohammed had been riddled with jiggers, a parasite that lives in dirt and eats away the flesh. It took all my nursing skills to sort that one out!

Willis helped me carry my bags. He's one of the older boys – as I write this he's nineteen now but still in school, where we are trying to catch him up on the years he has missed. He never had a father that he knew, but I can't help but notice how the smaller boys look up to him as an older brother, how he befriends them, and how sometimes the youngsters curl up on his lap and fall asleep.

Promises

As we drove away that day, I looked back at the cheering children and their smiling faces. Since the first visit in November 2009, so much had happened. I remembered the early visits as we interviewed children and looked through the reports from the social worker. Too often the words written down were 'rape', 'abuse' and 'torture'. And here they were. Now the word over their lives is 'rescued'.

From that first directive from God to look for land, through to the building process and the final opening, God had been faithful.

As we passed a family standing beside the dirt road, one of them shouted, 'Goodbye, Mama Bumala!'

I cried again.

Chapter Thirteen
Three Hours to Live

There were numerous trips back to Bumala B after the opening. There's one in particular that I remember.

As we drove back to Nairobi to catch our flight, Matt, my friend Brittany Perry and I were praying, thanking God for this latest mission trip, September 2014. It had been such fun – seeing the children doing so well at the children's home, catching up with Gerald and Florence and preaching in the local churches.

'And not even a serious mosquito bite!' announced Matt.

Back to the States

We were home for just a few days before the three of us, plus Josiah this time, flew out to the States. A few meetings in Ohio and Kentucky were planned, followed by a big fundraiser banquet in Mobile, Alabama, for OneByOne.

During those first meetings there was no hint of what we were about to face. The only thing that was odd, looking back, was Matt falling asleep in one or two of the car journeys. He never sleeps in the day and Brittany and I had fun teasing him about it.

'Matt! You're such a lightweight! We've done the same as you – Kenya, the States, the meetings . . . And here you are unable to stay awake!'

Our final meeting before the visit to Mobile for the fundraiser was a Sunday preach in Ohio. To facilitate this, we were staying the night at Brittany's house in Florence, Kentucky. The next morning, Matt was complaining of flu-like symptoms. We put it down to a cold or virus; Matt took some medication and we had a great Sunday meeting. It was only later when Matt said that he had struggled to keep going in the meeting – he had shown no sign of it and had spoken really well.

The next morning, as we said goodbye to Brittany and flew down to meet our friends Nick and Chelsea Jones, Matt was no better.

A trip to the doctor confirmed what I suspected. It was most likely some kind of viral infection. Matt was given some tablets and told to return in a couple of days if there was no improvement.

Things didn't improve. Matt was not eating or drinking properly so that by the day of the banquet on 2nd October, we were back to see Dr Mike Mahoney.

This time, Dr Mike ran some different tests while we stayed in the waiting room. A few minutes later he appeared with a frown on his face.

'There's something serious going on here. It looks like a severe infection of some sort. I've just phoned the hospital at Fairhope – they have a bed waiting for you, Matt.'

Hospital

It was a warm drive – not least because Matt was so cold he wouldn't let me put the air conditioning on. I dropped Matt off at the door of the hospital while I parked and got Josiah out of the car. By the time I got to the hospital reception, it was clear something was wrong.

Matt had collapsed as he approached the reception desk and had been violently sick. They had him in a wheelchair and a number of medical staff were surrounding him, asking him questions. One of the questions – repeated several times – was, 'Have you been to Africa recently?'

One of the doctors took me aside.

'Mrs Murray, we're sorry but your husband is showing all the symptoms of Ebola. As you have just come from Africa, we are going to have to treat Matthew as if he has the condition and put him into quarantine. We're very sorry.'

I tried to explain that we had been in East Africa and Ebola was happening in West Africa, thousands of miles away, but they were insistent on their processes. This was at a time when someone had recently come back to the States having contracted Ebola, so all the hospitals were on high alert.

Walking on the Moon

We were taken to a side room. At one point I looked through the window. What I saw was a shock. People were putting on enormous white suits, covering everything. It honestly looked like they were about to go on an expedition to walk on the moon.

I turned to Matt who had yet to see this.

'Matt, I don't want you to worry, but the people coming to put you in quarantine are wearing ridiculous suits like they are moon walking. It really is nothing. I think they're just overreacting.'

We stayed in the side room for a while longer while the suited-up nurses took swabs and did blood tests. A doctor – also dressed in the same way – came through with the results.

'Mr Murray, you have malaria. Can I ask you, did you take medication against malaria while you were in Africa?'

'Er, no.'

'Oh.'

'You see, Doctor, we've been to Kenya so many times and we've never had a problem. Our children in the home sometimes get malaria but they are fine after some medication.'

'I'm not sure this is the same type of malaria as those children,' said the doctor. 'We need to do some more tests.'

It was silly of us, I know. We had been rather naïve in not taking antimalarial medication. I'd like to say we did it in faith that God would protect – and we genuinely thought that because we travelled in Africa so often we had built up more resistance – but, honestly, we maybe had just become lax with our safety.

I was relieved, though, and whispered to Matt that after a few intravenous drips, he'd be fine!

The Banquet

The banquet still had to go ahead of course – just without Matt. I had to take over the role of speaking; something which I wasn't particularly comfortable about, but I had no choice.

All one hundred or so guests at the hotel in Mobile were very generous with their support of OneByOne that evening and I drove the hour back to Thomas Hospital, Fairhope, with a smile on my face. All was well and I was sure I was going to find that Matt's malaria had been properly diagnosed and medicated.

Josiah was still with me and as we walked into the hospital I could tell that something was not right. The nurses were pleasant but appeared to be avoiding answering my questions about my husband.

I was frustrated. Josiah was tired. Why couldn't I see Matt? What was the delay about?

Eventually a senior nurse came out to see me.

'Mrs Murray, we've put Matthew into strict isolation. We are still not sure whether this is Ebola. I'm sorry, but with your child here, you will not be able to see him.'

This really was overkill as far as I was concerned. I'm a straight-thinking nurse from Rotherham and this was an American hospital going paranoid over a simple case of malaria.

In the end I negotiated that we could wave at Matt through the window and Josiah was able to blow Daddy some kisses goodnight. Matt had his phone with him so I was able at least to text him and have a conversation that way.

I texted to say I'd be back in the morning without Josiah and hopefully would be able to see him then. And, with that, it was back to Nick and Chelsea's for the night.

Four in the Morning

It was only at four in the morning that I woke and remembered that one of the texts that Matt had sent me gave me the type of malaria he had contracted. I'd completely forgotten about this and had gone straight to bed when I'd got back. Now I was awake, I fired up the phone and googled the type – *Plasmodium falciparum*. I wasn't ready for what I read.

'The deadliest species . . . the disease's most dangerous form . . . Up to half a million deaths a year . . . Almost every malarial death is caused by this kind . . .'

Needless to say, I didn't go back to sleep.

As I ate some breakfast, a text came in from Matt:

'The doctors are worried about organ failure . . .'

By the time I arrived at the hospital a doctor was waiting to see me.

'Matthew's life is in the balance right now. We are seeing the early stages of organ failure – his heart, his lungs, his liver, his kidneys. We are moving him to Intensive Care.'

I started to pray under my breath, aware that this was going to be far more than a few days on antimalarials. My original optimism was swept away with that conversation.

I suited up and spent time with Matt, trying to keep him calm. That evening, I Facetimed Matt's parents and my parents in the UK to update them. Chelsea's mum came over to look after Josiah and Nick and Chelsea's two girls so that the next day – Friday by now – all three of us were able to travel in and visit Matt.

Crisis Point

Surely today would be better? That's what I was telling myself as Nick drove the three of us in.

Once we'd checked in, I found a doctor who was able to give me an update. Because I was a nurse, I tried to take in this information in the same way as I would with a handover of a patient on the ward in Rotherham. The only problem was, this was my husband.

Things had not improved. I suited up again and went in to see him. By now he was in and out of consciousness, and on the occasions when he was conscious he wasn't making a lot of sense. At one point, as I was quietly singing 'Amazing Grace' to him, he asked me whether I had written it.

Eventually the latest pathology results arrived, and with them the practitioner nurse – my main point of contact. Her name was Kathleen and I liked her a lot. She reminded me of myself. She was a very straight-forward nurse who both cared and remained professional.

'Matthew has deteriorated in the night. We now have the beginnings of organ failure on all his organs; it's getting worse and it's beginning to affect his brain. His platelet levels are dangerously low and he may therefore haemorrhage. His malaria infection level has increased from twenty per cent to nearly fifty per cent. This is at a fatal level. We are stopping the treatment now – there is nothing more we can do. Becky, we estimate your husband only has around three hours left to live. We will keep Matt on pain relief until he passes. I'm so sorry.'

I'd said to Nick and Chelsea that there was no need for them to come to the hospital with me, but at that moment I was so glad that they had. I collapsed into their arms and sobbed and sobbed.

Chapter Fourteen
Back From the Brink

I shook with the emotion of it all. Chelsea held me.

Nick was out in the corridor speaking to the staff. Or rather, shouting:

'Don't you quit on my friend! Let's get him transferred. Maybe the bigger hospital at Birmingham, Alabama, will know what to do. You can't just quit! You can't!'

At one point, Nick went in to see Matt and sneaked in his phone. This was not allowed, but while nurses were away, Nick Facetimed Nathan Morris and laid the phone on Matt's chest while Nathan prayed for a miracle.

Back in the side room I had started retching. My hands had pins and needles. I was uncontrollably sobbing; I felt it was the end, not just of our marriage but of our dreams.

I was blaming myself too. Kenya had always been my dream first. Matthew was there because of me.

I was the nurse. We hadn't taken the antimalarial tablets. That was my fault. When I saw Matt was ill, I had brushed it off. That was my fault. I had killed him . . .

Kathleen had been straight with me. She had said to me that with Matt's death, I had to stay home. I had a little boy of three who needed a mummy. I couldn't possibly go back to Africa.

It was said in Kathleen's straight-forward way, without judgement and with love.

And that's how it looked at that moment. I was about to lose my dreams, my Africa . . . my husband.

The Message

I stayed in the side room for quite a while. I knew I needed to be calm and assuring for Matt. As he drifted into consciousness, I wanted him to see my smile, not my hysteria. I wanted Matt's final moments to be peaceful. It took a while but in the end, and a pack or two of tissues later, I was ready to return to Matt's bedside.

Before I did, I pulled out my phone. I was very conscious of the need to update people and, even now, to ask for prayer.

With Nick's help, I sent out a message on Facebook:

'URGENT. Please pray for Matthew. His body is not responding to the drugs. Please join us in prayer right now!'

Nick added a #Pray4Matt graphic and photo, and off it went.

I had no idea at the time of the effect of this message. To me, it was an update on a dying husband. But to God's people, it acted as an SOS for urgent prayer. The message leapt from mobile to laptop, from friend to friend. People who didn't even know us began to pray. Later we learned that churches had stopped their usual meetings in order to spend time praying for Matt.

As the message and image travelled the world with thousands of 'shares', it reached Bethshan Church in Sunderland, the home of Ken and Lois Gott. They were meeting that night and turned the meeting into one of intercession for Matt. Luke Finch, who was leading the meeting, started to sing a refrain:

'Resurrection's in your veins, oh Matthew Murray, resurrection's in your veins, so don't you worry.'

It looks almost a childlike response as I see it written down, but God used it in an amazing way. For over thirty minutes, the whole church just kept on singing the phrase, again and again.

Over the next few hours, messages came in from the UK, USA, Canada, Germany, Spain, France, India, China, Australia, New Zealand, Thailand, Colombia, Brazil, Argentina, and from numerous countries in Africa. God's people were on the case!

As I sent the Facebook message, I knew none of that. I stiffened my resolve, blew my nose (again!) and began to walk down the corridor. The longest of walks to say goodbye to my husband. He was twenty-seven years old, a father to three-year-old Josiah, and about to go to glory.

The Smile

To get to Matt's room from the side room we were in, I had to go past the nurse's station. As I approached the duty nurse, she was smiling.

I couldn't quite work out what the smile meant though. It was an open, full on smile, not the kind gentle smile of condolence.

'Mrs Murray, I don't know if anyone has told you yet. We've just had some more results back. We have no idea why but the malaria levels in Matt's blood have gone down from fifty per cent to ten per cent.'

I stopped in my tracks and let out a wail; a cry, a shout, a scream all rolled into one.

Nick and Chelsea came running out of the side room and started to hold me, thinking the cry was one of anguish and that Matt had died.

'No, Nick, no,' I said, as I twisted away from him, 'it's not that! His levels are down! His levels are down!'

This wasn't super helpful information to Nick and Chelsea because if his platelet levels had dropped it was bad news.

'Which levels? Which levels?!' shouted Nick.

'It's his blood. His blood. The malaria levels have dropped!'

If God can do this, then . . .

Kathleen was waiting to talk to me. She was keen to bring a little realism to the newly found euphoria which had gripped me.

'Becky, there's a long way to go. Matt will almost certainly need kidney dialysis for the remainder of his life – his kidneys are in a really bad way. Other organs are affected. There are still toxins to deal with. There may be brain damage. I don't want you to think we are through it yet.'

I accepted Kathleen's assessment but inside I was shouting out hallelujahs. If God can bring Matt back from the brink, then surely He can completely heal him too? They didn't know why the malaria levels had dropped. But I knew why. And if the levels can drop supernaturally after treatment had ceased long before, then God can surely finish what He has started.

The Fifty Dollars

A week later, and Matt was still in Intensive Care; his organs were still in failure and, despite the miracle, by now I was frustrated and angry with the world. I'd been driving to the hospital every day, spending time with Matt, now fully conscious, but we'd been unable to see any further improvements.

Things came to a head one day when I was driving in. My friend Donna Williams had kindly given me her car to use while she was away. As I drove in the day before, the warning light had come on. A day later and I realised what it was – I was nearly out of fuel.

I had no cash on me and I'd left my credit card at Nick and Chelsea's. As I stopped at the traffic lights, I began to panic. I may have enough fuel to get to the hospital but it was most unlikely I'd get back again. Plus I had no money for food, or even a bottle of water.

Every emotion came to the surface at that moment. All the pent-up frustration. All the days of putting on brave faces. All the sleepless nights. All the assurances to Josiah that Daddy was going to be fine. Everything exploded.

A man drew up next to me at the lights, staring at me as I cried ugly tears. I was so grateful when the lights changed.

By the time I got to the hospital, I had composed myself and was ready to meet Matt in a better frame of mind. I was not sure how I was going to get home that day, but it was the afternoon's problem, not this morning's.

The Intensive Care Unit requires a check-in procedure for visitors and this can take a few minutes. While I was waiting, I sat in the reception area along with other anxious relatives, going through their own heartbreaking stories.

A lady approached me.

'Excuse me, I have absolutely no idea why, but I feel compelled to give you this.'

And with that, she handed over fifty dollars. A few moments later and we had gone our separate ways. I never saw her again. But at that moment, I knew. I knew for sure Matt would be well. I heard the whisper of the Holy Spirit telling me, 'I've got this.' And He had.

Through the smallest of gestures, through the money for a tank of fuel with enough left over for a coffee, God had sent me the assurance I needed. If God is in the detail, how much more the bigger issues? I no longer doubted. Matt would be well.

God's Protection

I'm still learning. I will always be learning more about God and His ways this side of eternity. But I learned something precious that day through the kindness of a lady. I learned that even in the hardest of times, God protects us.

One of my favourite stories is that of Paul in Acts 28 in the Bible. He's being taken to Rome to face trial and on the way he gets shipwrecked. Worse than that, after he has helped save the passengers he is bitten by a snake. Despite that, God protects him – so much so that his fellow passengers start to say he must be a god because he didn't die from the snake bite. From a criminal to a god in one moment!

I love that even in the hardest of circumstances, God was protecting Paul. In the hardest of circumstances Matt and I have had to face so far in our lives, He protected us.

In seeing how God cared that I had fuel in the car, I saw how much He cared for us with the bigger issue of Matt's health. I saw how He loved and protected us even through the hardest of times.

Paul says, 'The Lord is faithful. He will establish you and guard you against the evil one' (2 Thessalonians 3:3). That's the truth for all of us. If, like me, you go through hard times, if you have impossible situations, if right now you need God's care and protection, why not pray this prayer with me:

'Lord, thank You that You love me. Jesus, thank You that You died for me. Thank You that You care for me. I ask for that care right now in the situation I'm going through. I trust You for the outcome. I believe You are faithful. And I believe that You protect me. Be with me now, Lord. Amen.'

Routine

Matt was still far from well. Thankfully, by now the authorities had decided he didn't have Ebola, but his organs had all failed to some extent and we were continuing to pray on a daily basis for recovery. I developed a routine over the days that followed.

First, a call to the hospital as soon as I woke to check on Matt. Then a call or a Facetime to Matt's parents, then mine. Then a drive to the hospital and a morning with Matt. Home for lunch with Josiah and a fun afternoon with him, trying to keep things as normal as possible for a three-year-old; maybe swimming, shopping or going for a meal. Then back to the hospital. Then home in the evening, put Josiah to bed, and finally back to the hospital for a third visit.

My daily treat on the way home after that third visit was to call in at a fast food place over the road from the hospital and buy an 'M&Ms ice-cream blast' – a large cup full of ice cream infused with M&Ms. A heavenly end to each tiring day – though I must admit, I did put on a bit of weight! Actually I got one each for Nick and Chelsea most nights as well and the three of us would eat them at home as it neared midnight, watching episodes of *House* on television. I'm not sure why I was watching a medical drama when I had enough medical dramas of my own though.

I remember one day passing a shop that had a plaque for sale. The plaque read, 'The will of God will never take you where the grace of God will not keep you.' I bought it and if you visit our home anytime, you'll see it on our living-room wall. Seeing it for the first time was a beautiful moment. I needed to know that truth at that particular instant, and God showed it to me in a shop – not even a Christian shop as far as I know.

Matt's body slowly began to pull through. First the enlarged heart went back to its proper size. Then the partially collapsed lungs recovered. Then the liver showed up as normal.

The kidneys were the main problem. The initial diagnosis was that they would never recover and Matt would need to make use of a dialysis machine for the rest of his life. It was an amazing day when the nurse came through to Matt's room to ask if she could take the machine away as he didn't need it any more. It was just ten days after Matt had been told that he'd probably be on dialysis for life and may even need a kidney transplant. The dialysis machine was wheeled away and Matt's kidneys were declared normal.

Recovery

When eventually Matt's medical reports were shown to Dr Mike Mahoney, the doctor who had first seen Matt, he declared that 'there is no medical explanation for Matthew's recovery'.

The recovery continued. There were precious visits to the hospital from Ken Gott and Nathan Morris over the next few weeks, both of which helped to encourage us. Earlier Pastor Cleddie Keith had come too. He took two planes and hired a car, all at his own expense, just to put his arms around me and pray. He'd check I'd eaten, buy me a meal if I hadn't and just be for me the dad I needed so far away from home.

The malaria eventually disappeared completely from Matt's bloodstream and at this point he was transferred off Intensive Care. I was grateful, but sad to miss my straight-speaking nurse friend Kathleen.

A couple of final postscripts to this unwanted adventure. One of the nurses, Stephanie, had been quietly observing us and our friends. She couldn't compute our response to the condition. She was impressed by our faith in God, and eventually we had the privilege of praying a prayer with her, asking Jesus to change her life.

One year later, we went back to Thomas Hospital to thank the staff. As we walked in, there was Kathleen. I hadn't realised but since we were originally there she had started following us on social media, so the first thing she said that day, after having previously counselled me to give up on Africa, was, 'I get it now.'

A precious moment.

Chapter Fifteen
South and East

'So where is it again we're going?'

Matt's driving, it's Sunday morning and I've not been paying attention.

'Uttoxeter. David Owen is the pastor. He and his wife Averil have asked us to speak.'

'Ah yes. So kind of them to let us talk about OneByOne.'

The Meetings

The meeting went well. Matt preached. I spoke about our charity. We went out for lunch with David and Averil, and then it was time to leave.

'Thank you so much for coming,' said David. 'We've been talking as a board. As you know, I will be retiring and we'd like to ask the two of you to take over the pastoring of the church.'

Matt burst out laughing. Maybe not the best response.

'That's so kind of you to ask us,' said Matt, 'but really, pastoring is not for us. We're far too involved with OneByOne.'

And that was it. Off we went back to Rotherham.

We should have seen the signs earlier. David mentioning a number of times in various conversations that he was retiring. Significant and deep conversations during the morning with members of the board at Uttoxeter Pentecostal Church. Insistence that we should preach there.

But we didn't see those signs and were taken by surprise.

We were back there two months later. Again, in my naïvety, I assumed they liked the work we were doing with OneByOne.

It was only in the car park afterwards that I realised there was another agenda. This time, David and Averil approached me. Maybe they thought I'd be the easier one to persuade – little do they know it's Matt who is the softer touch!

'Becky, we want you to know that we still think you and Matt are the ones to take the church on. We've been praying about it and we're so convinced it's you, we haven't even begun approaching anyone else. Please will you pray about it and consider it?'

I said we were flattered to be asked. And I said 'no'. I was clear that we were very busy with the charity and travelling extensively.

As we drove back up the A50, I was laughing about it with Matt.

'Here was me thinking they were super keen on OneByOne and on your preaching! But they wanted us to consider pastoring there!'

Matt turned to me as we drove.

'Becky, I hope we've not missed God here.'

'No, Darling, of course not! How could this possibly be the plan of God for us?'

'But, Becky, honestly. Maybe we should have at least prayed about it. We've just said 'no' without even consulting God.'

Green Light

We agreed we would both go away and pray about it. I remember thinking that this might be a short prayer. Surely God would not want us as pastors with all we were doing on the mission field?

But a funny thing happened. A week or so later, Matt and I compared notes. We had both felt the prompting of the Holy Spirit that this was actually the call of God and we should accept the invitation.

We decided to do one more thing to test out whether this really was from God. We decided to do nothing further, but if it really was God's will for us to go to Uttoxeter, the church would contact us a third time.

Sure enough, a week later we got an email from one of the board members once again asking us to consider the position of pastors of the church.

We said yes. They were as shocked as we were that we agreed!

The church was still under the old rules of the Assemblies of God denomination. That meant that the whole church had to vote for us to go there. That meant a third trip to Uttoxeter and a third preach for Matt. This time, though, it was more like a job interview.

I remember part way through the meeting, as we were taking communion, Matt got his mobile out. Matt is renowned for forever texting on his phone, but I was cross.

'Matt, put your phone away! You can't be texting during communion! What will the church think?'

Little did I know, Matt had received a Holy Spirit prompt to text someone with a word from God. Nevertheless, it didn't look good. So there we were in the middle of communion, having a mini 'domestic' as to whether Matt could text whilst being observed by the rest of the church who were about to take a vote as to whether we should be the new pastors. It all seemed a bit surreal.

Waiting

By now we really wanted the job! We had turned a full 180 degrees from our original position. I remember we were in Sri Lanka on the Sunday when the church would be voting. Sri Lanka is five and a half hours ahead of UK time. Therefore, by the time we were expecting to hear the result we would have completed three Sunday services, enjoyed vast amounts of Sri Lankan hospitality and be winding down near the end of the day.

The problem was, we weren't winding down at all. We were on edge awaiting the result. It felt like an exam.

The text arrived. The role was offered. We accepted, of course, and started serving at Uttoxeter Pentecostal Church in January 2015.

There was one glitch . . . The first part of this story, up to and including the offer, was just before a certain mission trip to Kenya. Just before Matt started fighting for his life. At one point in this story, I had composed an email to the church in Uttoxeter telling them that sadly their new pastor had just died . . . By God's grace I never had to send it.

Paratroopers

We have loved, and continue to love, serving in Uttoxeter. In 2017, we changed the name to Renew Church, Uttoxeter. And we're grateful for the growth over the time we have been there, seeing the congregation more than double.

Early on, our good friend Pastor Cleddie Keith visited. While he was here, he brought a couple of prophecies that we felt were very relevant. The first was that God would bring paratroopers to us – spiritual paratroopers. Men and women on fire for God would be joining us.

The second prophetic word was that God would send a good number of South Africans to us.

God answered both prophecies in a wonderful way and, to an extent, the two words from God merged into one.

At the time Cleddie was here, we had only one South African family in the church. Today we have over thirty. They join a growing army of loving followers of Jesus. By God's grace, we have over two hundred in our Sunday meetings – men and women who are on fire for God – all of them, from the UK and many other nations, spiritual paratroopers.

Every Household

Our passion is that every single household in Uttoxeter would know that God loves them, that we reach every resident from the youngest to the oldest. With this in mind, we now work into all the primary schools on a regular basis, as well as some of the middle schools, and we regularly visit all the care homes.

We've done some pretty crazy things over the years. Last year we ran a Mission Week for Uttoxeter. It was important for Matt and me that we not only reach people through OneByOne around the world, but that equally, we reach and serve everyone where we live. We wanted to run a Mission Week for Uttoxeter on the same basis as the Mission Weeks we run in Kenya or Sri Lanka, so we asked the whole church to give up time for the week and treat it just as if they were on a team in another country.

One particularly sunny Saturday afternoon in the summer of 2019, we hired a small plane to fly over the town. Behind it, it carried a massive banner that said 'Jesus Loves Uttoxeter – Renew Church'. So many people were out in their gardens that day and we received comments about it for weeks afterwards. One family in particular responded to it and came along to church the following day. They are still with us.

Just as Jesus washed the feet of the disciples, we wanted to wash the feet of the whole town. In addition to telling people about Jesus, we wanted to serve and show Jesus. We ended up literally washing the town! We washed down road signs, we did car washes for free, we cleaned up streets and gardens and we renewed a number of gardens for older people and single mums.

God is giving us influence in the town, and we have strong connections with a number of the local politicians and council leaders. Our own MP found a living faith in Jesus through a connection with Matt. Matt was able to help him with a number of personal issues in his life at the time. We are reaching a great cross-section of the town with the gospel of Christ and have seen a good number pray to ask Jesus to change their life.

We love the faithfulness of our church people. We love that they treat every day as a day to speak about Jesus and a day to serve the town. We unashamedly say 'thank you' to them in this book. We love every one of them and are excited to be sharing the journey with them.

All this in Uttoxeter! A small market town stuck between Stoke and Derby. In fact, when I first heard we were going to visit I had rather got my town names muddled up and thought we were driving down to Devon – but that's Exeter!

A New Country

Just as we moved south for our local church, so we were moving east with our missions.

When I first heard God's directions on mission, I assumed it would only be Kenya. In fact I assumed I would be moving there in a traditional missionary role. But things changed. The way we were working in Kenya allowed us to think bigger and look further.

Soon after arriving in Uttoxeter, I began to get the country of Sri Lanka in my head each time I prayed about missions. Which was a little odd, as I knew nothing about the country and knew no one there. I tried to put the thought to one side as there seemed no way we could be involved there. But I did begin to feel that it must be a 'God-prompt' for no other reason than I couldn't be making it up!

It was about this time that we were due to go over to Cleddie's church in Kentucky to speak there. The flights had already been booked when we got a phone call from Cleddie's PA.

'Becky, I'm really sorry . . . We've never done this before, but we've managed to double book you for the Friday night service you and Matt were speaking at. I'm so sorry.'

'No problem. We'll come anyway as the flights are booked – and it's not a wasted trip as we're speaking at another church not far from you on the Sunday.'

So off we went. We quite enjoyed the thought of just being with Cleddie and his church and not having to speak.

When we got to the Friday-night service, we found out who they had double booked us with: Vernon Perera, the Assemblies of God overseer for the whole of . . . Sri Lanka.

Two months later, we're arriving in Colombo as guests of Vernon, staying at his house.

War Widows

As we talked with Vernon, I felt a particular drawing to the widows he described. In Jaffna, on the northern tip of Sri Lanka, there were many widows as a result of the civil war, which had lasted over twenty years and only finished in 2009. Our discussions led to an introduction to Pastor Sam.

Now in his seventies, Pastor Sam is a remarkable man. He chose to stay in the Jaffna war zone throughout the civil war, despite invites to work at churches in the States and Australia. Throughout the war, and in spite of the war, Pastor Sam was able to plant over one hundred new churches.

One of the most memorable and heartbreaking moments on our Sri Lanka trip was a visit to a beach. It looked idyllic but, as we approached, Pastor Sam warned us to beware of the bones we would find. The beach had been closed for a long time, and only recently reopened. It was the beach at the centre of a massacre of civilians near the end of the war in 2009. To this day, human bones are commonly found there.

By the end of our visit with Pastor Sam, we knew what we were called to do. For the first year we ran a feeding programme for the widows and their children. There were so many widows, some of them younger than me. And their stories were horrific.

One lady was particularly traumatised. In order to escape from the troops, she carried her twins across an estuary, but got into trouble in the water. She had to face the fact that, to survive, she would have to let go of one of her twins to save the other. She made a decision no mother should ever have to make. I prayed and cried with her, as God began to wash away the guilt she still felt over the decision she had had to make.

Hope Sri Lanka

As we worked with the widows, we developed the feeding programme and gave it a name – Hope Sri Lanka. So many of the women had given up any hope of enjoying life again. They lived off scraps, trying to make ends meet to provide for their children, and were simply surviving.

Most of the widows were from a Hindu or Buddhist background. In order to pick up their regular food parcels, they were asked first to attend a church service. The parcels were given out at the end of the service. Many beautiful widow women have found salvation in Jesus Christ as a result.

The feeding programme dealt with the key needs at the point we arrived, but it closed in 2019. We have established seven sewing centres for the widows, in order to take them on beyond 'survival' to living again and earning an income. This restores hope and confidence.

The first products, which came out in August 2017, were simple cloth shopping bags, many of which were made from old pillow cases and other discarded cotton items. The production of the bags coincided with a government decision to ban plastic bags, so the timing was perfect.

Today the ladies do much more. They make dresses and other clothes, all of which can be sold through markets and local businesses. There are over a hundred ladies working in this business.

We are now beginning to work in the city of Colombo too – especially after the Easter bombings in 2019 where, as a result, there are new widows and orphans.

Carriers of Hope

Hope is the appropriate name for the work in Sri Lanka. There seemed to be no hope. The widows were lost and forgotten by those around them. But God had not forgotten them and with the new programme there is real hope.

From the manufacture of carrier bags, we have seen these wonderful ladies become carriers of hope themselves.

Paul speaks about hope in Colossians 1:26-27: '[Called to make known] the mystery hidden for ages and generations but now revealed to his saints. To them God chose to make known how great among the Gentiles are the riches of the glory of this mystery, which is Christ in you, the hope of glory.'

Paul says, 'Christ in you, the hope of glory.' That's Christ our hope in you, not Christ in your pastor, not Christ in the evangelist, but Christ in you! We are to be carriers of hope in what can sometimes feel like a very hopeless world.

Paul writes in Romans 5:5: 'Hope does not put us to shame, because God's love has been poured into our hearts through the Holy Spirit who has been given to us.'

Ordinarily when we use the word hope, we express uncertainty rather than certainty. We hope the bus will come on time, we hope that the business meeting won't drag on too long. But biblical hope is a confident expectation. It's anchored on a truth that is unwavering. So it's not a wishful uncertainty where we cross our fingers and wish for the best, but it's a surety, a quiet confidence in Jesus. Hope in God can never fail.

May I encourage you to carry hope. May I encourage you to allow the Holy Spirit to affirm within you the fact that as Christians we have a certain hope. It can overcome the seemingly impossible. Just ask the ladies in Sri Lanka.

Chapter Sixteen
Dignity

With the work growing, I was in and out of Kenya on a regular basis. In addition to the children's home, we have been able to develop a school. We now employ skilled teachers who teach from the national curriculum in a Christian environment. King's School has exceeded its expectations, coming first in our region in the exam league tables, and wealthier families have started paying to send their children there.

As always, we want to do all we can to bring Christ to everyone we meet. We work with outreach teams, partnering with Bill Wilson's organisation Metro World Child. This enables us to reach over 10,000 children every week through our schools' programme.

Dignity Project

One of the most far-reaching projects is the Dignity Project.

One day, a lady approached me in Bumala B. 'Sister Becky, please will you pray for my daughter? She's been missing for three months.'

Within days, another lady approached me: 'Please pray for my missing child. My daughter has been gone for five months now.'

As I asked more questions, it became clear what had happened.

Here, right on the doorstep of King's School, right in the village of Bumala B and the surrounding villages, sex traffickers were at work.

What could we do?

The Dignity Project was born.

I noticed that girls often missed a week of school each month due to their periods, meaning they lose a vital part of their education. By the end of their schooling, they have missed up to a quarter of their education. It means they don't have the grades to get a good job. And, tragically, this is when they are most vulnerable to offers that come along – offers that seem too good to be true. Because they are. And as a result, we lose them to sex trafficking.

Surely it couldn't be too hard to help them? Can't we help them? Can't we reach them before the traffickers do?

Over time, we began to develop Dignity Days. These days were educational – not just relating to the girls' monthly period but to the real danger of trafficking. With education, girls can be aware in advance of what to look for, who to avoid and where to report any attempted abductions. Where possible, representatives from the police and local government are also in attendance to support our staff, particularly in reference to sexual abuse warnings.

We developed Dignity Bags which are given to every girl that goes through the Dignity Project. Girls receive four re-usable sanitary products. Developed in Uganda, the pads are washable and can last for up to a year. Dignity Bags also include two pairs of underwear and information about trafficking. Bags are given out at the end of each Dignity Day along with food and refreshments for the girls.

I met a councillor called Mary in Kenya who told me she had met girls using rags, old tissues and even cow dung through their cycles. Cow dung is very absorbent and so the girls had attempted to use this as they couldn't afford pads. You can only imagine the infections this caused.

In March 2019, the Dignity Project was officially launched at the Houses of Parliament in the UK, with several MPs and delegates attending. I shared how our goal was to reach 20,000 girls by the end of 2020.

The event was supported and attended by the Minister for International Development, Harriett Baldwin MP, who observed that the Dignity Project completely aligned with the government's own aims to end 'period poverty'. The Dignity Project today works in a number of countries, including Kenya, Uganda, South Africa, Sierra Leone, Pakistan, India, Brazil, Zambia and Zimbabwe.

Brazil is one of our newer initiatives.

Sex and Violence

We knew it would be tough. We were taking a team into one of the most difficult parts of São Paulo, Brazil. But the way had opened for the Dignity Project to meet some of the children. One of them was Perma. When we met her, she was fifteen years old.

Perma grew up in a home where domestic violence was the norm. For years she wondered why her mum put up with it until she was old enough to realise that this was the only way her mum knew to keep a roof over her and her little brothers' heads.

Perma went to school but there was only one route home. This was via an isolated path and past a large tree where a gang would wait. Each and every day they would gang rape her. At first Perma didn't say anything, thinking it would be too distressing for her mum. Eventually, though, she told her father.

'Perma, you're a girl. That's just what happens!'

Perma was both shocked and heartbroken by her dad's response, and the result was she began to self-harm. She simply couldn't deal with what was happening to her. Finally, Perma told her mum. Her mother was furious with her father and threw him out of the home. For a little while life was better.

A few months later, her father came back promising life would be different. In front of her mother he was sweet and kind with Perma, but every time her mother left the house he would beat Perma and even held her hand over the fire to hurt her. One day her father did the unimaginable. He invited the gang from the tree around, where he allowed them to violate Perma in her own home.

When her mum found out, she reported this to the police and now both the gang and her father are serving prison sentences.

Perma's scars were both physical and emotional. For a long time she continued to self-harm. She felt lost and was not able to believe that she had any future.

But the day came when the Dignity Project came to her school. Perma couldn't believe that finally someone was telling girls that it was not acceptable to be treated by men in this way and that their bodies were not for sale.

There are over 2,500 prostitutes living within a one-mile radius in São Paulo, Brazil. It has even become a tourist area because of the amount of sex workers available. And because prostitution is so rife in this culture, boys view girls as possessions to take as and when they please.

Our team were able to lead sessions with both the boys and girls. We empowered the girls as to how to protect themselves and encouraged the boys in what it means to be a real man. We talked to the boys about the impact of pornography and why it should be avoided. We talked of human trafficking and the sexual crimes that go with it.

The Dignity Project is so needed. Perma's smile that day showed why.

Kenya Again

Despite the new initiatives, Matt and I have continued to invest into all we are doing in Kenya. The school is now well established next to the children's home and we are seeing the beginnings of a whole village transformed. Not least the local witch doctor.

I first met Elizabeth on one of our early visits. We had the privilege of leading her to a faith in Christ. It was then that we learned that Elizabeth was the wife of the local witch doctor. She was so bold with her new-found faith, not afraid to confront her husband. I was concerned though. I wasn't sure he would react well to Elizabeth finding a faith in Christ. So much so, I decided a visit was in order.

The first person I noticed when I got to the house was Devine. Devine was one of our new day students. God has given us such favour as a school, we are finding many in the villages want to send their children to us. I hadn't appreciated, though, who Devine's father was!

I was well received by him and he allowed me to share my faith. As I talked, I began to notice tears in his eyes. By the end of my time with him, he had also prayed a prayer, asking Jesus to change him. The witch doctor is a witch doctor no more!

Leonard is one of our children who I have seen change the most. He came to us severely traumatised from daily beatings by his mother. Over the years that followed, we have seen him develop into a lovely young man, full of faith in Christ. So much so, he has asked to go back home and speak to his mother of his faith. This was the woman who daily beat him. And he loves her still – enough to share the gospel with her.

Mauko

At the end of one of our Kenya visits and with the main team having gone, Brittany and I had a couple of days to spare before our own flight home. Brittany had met a lady at one of our clinics who had asked for help with her house – the roof was falling down. Admittedly, neither of us felt particularly able with roof building, but we went along to see if we could help.

The woman lived a couple of villages away, in the village of Mauko. We were aware of Mauko's reputation. It was known as a murder capital among the villages. Others spoke of the Mauko villagers as having 'blood in their blood', so frequent were the murders and maimings. The police were nervous to go there and one gang in particular dominated village life.

That was the atmosphere we walked into that day. We found the lady's house, who turned out not to be there anyway, but immediately noticed something else.

Sitting on a chair outside one of the huts was a little girl, Brenda. Brenda was eight years old and the first thing we noticed were her arms. They were so thin. But her stomach was distended. At first I thought it was malnutrition, but on closer examination her legs and lower body looked quite healthy. It was clear that there was something seriously wrong.

We spoke with the girl's mother but she was hesitant to do anything. We offered to take Brenda to a hospital, to pay for the transport and to pay for accommodation for the mother as well. Still the hesitation.

It was at this moment the older brother joined the conversation. He was rude and aggressive. He made it clear that he didn't trust us and, in any case, Brenda had just been to the witch doctor, so it was best to leave things for a while to see if there was improvement.

We later learned that the older brother was part of the gang that ruled the village.

Eventually we got permission to take Brenda to the local hospital. She was diagnosed with Burkitt's lymphoma, a cancer of the immune cells; her distended stomach was due to a large tumour growing in her abdomen. The doctors told us of a hospital close to Nairobi that could offer her the treatment for this cancer. We jumped at the opportunity and offered to pay all of the hospital bills. But no sooner were we on the plane back to England than the family took Brenda back home, refusing the offer of treatment. Brenda died just a few days later on 3rd March 2016.

The Call to Do More

I couldn't get Brenda out of my mind. The whole situation in Mauko seemed so dire. It's not a village that would have immediately been on our map in terms of outreach. Matt and I are clear that we serve well in the places we have been called to and only move further on once we feel that the first work is well established. And even then, we would have been reaching out to other villages nearer to Bumala B before we got to Mauko.

But it was Mauko and Brenda that wouldn't leave my mind.

The more I learned of Mauko, the more I was praying for it. I learned more on the fact it was a murder capital of the region. I learned that there had been four murders and a gang rape within the last few weeks. I learned there had been a suicide by hanging. I learned that the gang were petrifying the locals, often killing for no reason. I learned that witchcraft was particularly strong in Mauko.

Having discovered more, I asked Matt whether I could go back! Matt was supportive, but there was no surprise in his suggestion that it should wait for the next trip when he would be with me. And so it was.

In fact it was the first trip with members from Renew Church, Uttoxeter. There was no doubting we were throwing our church in the deep end in terms of ministry. First-timers, and we were taking them to the darkest possible place we knew in Kenya!

It was not just the Uttoxeter team. For the first time we took Josiah with us to Africa. He was five. I was nervous about this. With Matt and me so active, it would be easy for someone with malice to take Josiah in a moment. We prayed a lot in preparation for this particular trip.

The Market Place

It was a hot day. No clouds and a late-afternoon sun beating down.

Noisy too. Ladies selling tomatoes to one side of the square. On the other side are the taxi motorbikes, together with a crowd of men – the drivers waiting for business.

In the middle of this noise, colour and activity, we all pitched up. Me and Matt, Josiah, the team from Uttoxeter and a good number of our children. This was our children's choir, and a good way to attract attention. We stood near the middle of the square and the children started to sing.

Immediately the ladies selling their tomatoes turned to look at us. A few took steps towards us, seemingly entranced by the children's voices. There was less movement from the men but more than one stopped their conversations. One man blew smoke from the last of his cigarette, threw it to the floor and, with hands in pockets, walked towards us.

A crowd began to gather. At the end of the singing, Matt shared the love of Jesus, with one of our local staff translating. The noise in the square lessened and hand after hand was raised – dear, lost people, caught up in one of the most difficult places on the planet to live, each raising a hand to say that they wanted Jesus to change their life.

In two days, sixty-two people committed their lives to Christ.

Then the miracles started.

One little girl who had been partially blind, and had had to make use of large-print books at school, was completely healed. We got her to read the very small print of a local Bible. Word perfect.

An older man, who had been unable to work on his local allotment because of the pain in his back, was healed and demonstrated it by stretching down to the floor and back again. It meant that there would be food on the table once more, with him being able to work the land.

On one of the days, we revisited Brenda's family. Sadly, they were not interested in talking to us but we saw the neighbour looking on, so went over to talk to her. Her name was Maggie. And Maggie was angry.

'How can you dare come here and talk about the love of God! He does not love me! Today is the anniversary of my child's death. Where was He then? How can you say He loves me?'

One of my team moved forward and held the lady's hand. Rachel had lost her soldier brother in war. With tears in her eyes, Rachel shared with Maggie how she had come to a choice – a choice where she had to decide whether to lean in to God or run from God because of what had happened. Rachel made her choice and God met her in a beautiful way.

As Rachel spoke, Maggie began to cry. The tears turned into deep sobs as Maggie cried out that she needed help.

That day, she found it. Maggie prayed with us and asked Jesus to come into her life. Now she is one of our Sunday school workers.

But the story doesn't end there. Maggie's husband was sceptical as to what had happened and said to Maggie that he would only believe when he saw real change.

We noticed that he had sores on his legs. As one of the motorbike taxi drivers, this was a particular problem for him. He couldn't get on the bike without severe pain.

Maggie began to pray for him regularly.

Six months later, we are back in their house and we ask the husband whether he will now come to Christ.

'If I see real change I will.'

'How are your legs, by the way?'

'You know, they are so much better! Thank you for asking.'

'That's great. Did you get some medication for them then?'

'No, actually. They seem to have cleared up on their own.'

Maggie smiled and said, 'You know I have been praying for you every day? I've been praying for your healing.'

His mouth dropped open. That was the proof he needed and that afternoon we had the privilege of praying with him and introducing him to Jesus Christ. The children came to Christ too, and we had the joy of seeing the whole family in church every week.

The Tree and the Bench

Yes, church.

When we started seeing so many finding a faith in Christ, we decided we needed to do something about it. We set up church in the market square. In the middle of the square there is a tree with a bench underneath it. The bench became our pulpit each Sunday as we gathered.

As we preached every Sunday, it was fun to see the congregation move around us as the sun moved and they stayed under the shade of the tree.

The noise and bustle of the square continued even on the Sunday, so it was a noisy scene too. But at the same time, it was an open declaration of what Jesus had done for the village of Mauko.

Today we have a plot of land and a church building. Around a hundred people attend each week. Since we first arrived in August 2016 right through to today, there hasn't been one murder in Mauko.

The people that had 'blood in their blood' have been washed in Jesus' blood.

Stephen

One of the people you will always see at the front of Mauko church on Sunday is Stephen. He arrived with us in an unusual way.

Stephen had been an alcoholic. He was wandering through the village late one night when the pastors were holding an all-night prayer meeting. They saw him and invited him in, as it simply wasn't safe in the village that late at night. Stephen came in and the next day, 9th December 2017, still slightly hungover, he gave his life to Christ.

The drinking stopped straight away. Because he was no longer drinking and no longer spending money on prostitutes, there was money again for his family. His wife, who had been planning to divorce him, didn't do so. His children had the food and clothes they needed. They can go to school now because the money is there to pay for their education.

Stephen has now trained as a school teacher and is one of the main helpers in the church. A life transformed; a family transformed. Because we stopped for the one.

The Gang

The fact that there have been no further murders is a talking point of the village even to today. The gang behind many of the killings still exists, but have simply been less effective in their terrorising of the villagers.

I wanted to reach the gang.

One day a few of us walked over to where the gang were mainly based. They weren't there, but one of the wives was, and we got talking.

As soon as we started to talk to her, she began to cry. We asked her why.

The lady opened her hand to reveal a small bottle. It was poison. She had been about to take her life.

For her, things had got too much. Being married to one of the gang leaders meant that she was shunned by the rest of the village. No one would talk to her, whether that was out of fear or loathing. And she had had enough.

We were able to pray with her that afternoon and introduce her to life on the day she had intended death.

Mauko is no longer a dark place. All because of meeting a little girl called Brenda.

Chapter Seventeen
The Overflow

With successful and established missions in Kenya and Sri Lanka, I was happy just to continue with these, bearing in mind the success of the broader Dignity Project, but I felt God prompting me with regard to one other country. Pakistan.

Eternal Fruit

I had first considered Pakistan way back in 2006 when I was working with Nathan Morris. I felt that God was telling me that one day I would work there, that the work would be different to what I would do in other nations but that the results would be just as good. And that the fruit from the work would last into eternity.

I was encouraged by God's promise, but aware at the time that it wasn't a 'now' word; nor was I entirely sure it was 'my' word. I thought that it may well be a word for Nathan and Shake the Nations as they were the team I was working for at the time – but it turned out to be for me and OneByOne. By the time the opportunity arose in Pakistan, I'd forgotten all about God's prompt those years ago – but of course, God hadn't forgotten!

The opening came via the Dignity Project. We had been talking to the Elim church movement about partnering with some of their missionaries and one of the couples we were introduced to were Arham and Katherine from Pakistan.

I went out to take a look at what they were doing and to discuss the Dignity Project. My mum wasn't too happy with me going to what she perceived to be a dangerous country for Christians to work in. I assured her it was just a four-day trip and there would be no further need for me to travel there. Little did I know!

The Brick Factories

The Dignity Project went so well. Working with a local church, we reached 1,100 girls. Many of them over the four days gave their lives to Christ and the church was able to do the follow up – the reason why we always insist on working with churches on the ground.

On the final day of the trip, we went to visit a brick factory. This was something Arham had been talking about over the time we were there.

I wasn't ready for what I would see.

It was because of Arham's relationship with the owners that we were able to get in. What we saw was horrific.

My only connection with the modern slave trade had been through girls who had been trafficked for sex. Everyone knew it was wrong and tried to hide what they were doing.

There was no hiding what was happening in this factory. As we walked in, there in front of us were hundreds of families. All of them slaves. All of them working to produce bricks.

There are no chains around them, but they cannot leave the site. Their identity documents are removed when they go into the factories. The brick masters own them. Mothers, fathers, children, aunts, uncles. Even elderly grandparents. All of them working from first light to dusk, producing bricks.

Why are they there? They have voluntarily sold themselves into slavery to help solve financial debts. In Pakistan, debts are often inherited. We met children paying off grandparents' debts. Comparatively small amounts (to our eyes) can lead to whole families working for the rest of their lives as bonded labour in the brick factories.

Interest Rate

Through Arham translating, I asked a young couple why they were there. The man explained that after marriage, they were pregnant with their first child. But there were complications and a C-section was needed. The banks would not provide the money and even if they were to consider a loan, it could take months. The money was needed straight away. So they did the only thing open to them – borrowed the money from a brick master. And here they were, years later, with three more children, still paying off the debt.

The amount of the loan for the surgery? The equivalent of US$150.

I am talking to the family thirteen years after this loan. I'm incredulous.

'But surely by now you have paid off the $150 loan? It's thirteen years ago!'

'No, madam,' says the man through Arham translating. 'We now owe $2,500. The interest is so high we never get to pay it off. And if we don't make our quota of bricks in a day, we have to borrow money to eat that night.'

It turns out that even their youngest four-year-old girl has a quota of bricks to complete in a day. Any of their four children failing to make the required quota will extend the loan.

I was almost in tears. Shocked at the blatancy of the open slavery. I whispered to Arham.

'Is there any way we can pay the $2,500 and redeem them? I'm sure I could do a fundraiser for them. We can't do it for everyone, but how about we start with this family?'

Arham smiled.

'Becky, it's only $2,500 for them to pay. If they see it is you, they will simply put the money up four or five times to outprice you. The family are worth too much to the brick master for him to let them go.'

Walking Back to Slavery

Arham explained to me later that on one occasion, someone had successfully redeemed a family. The problem was that the family, once released, had no home and no job. The only thing they knew how to do was to make bricks.

A week after their release, they voluntarily walked back into the factory.

As I listened to the story, all of a sudden I realised why the Israelites had wanted to go back to Egypt after Moses had set them free. They wanted the security. They wanted their homes. They wanted what they knew. They were willing to walk back into slavery.

Working in Egypt can be very tempting for all of us. If we are to step out of what is keeping us in slavery, it needs to be with faith and understanding that we have a bond-breaking God who not only sets us free, but sets us on a new course. He will provide for us.

Whatever it is we feel enslaved by today, pray with me that God would not only break the bonds of the slavery, the addiction, the lifestyle, but also show us how to live in freedom, trusting Him for our everyday needs.

A New Home

On the flight back home, I was unsettled. Matt and I were discussing what we had witnessed in Pakistan.

'Matt, what if we build a home for the children of the brick factories? What if we give the parents access whenever they want? At least that way we get the children out of slavery.'

'Yes, Babe, but that's so opposite to what we have done in Kenya. We never want to take the child away from the parent.'

'But if we don't, Matt, we are doing nothing. That four-year-old girl will never get an education. She will never be free. She will live and die a slave next to the brick kilns.'

My mind was whirring with the thought. If we could secure the release of the children, they then get an education. If they get an education, then they can get a well-paid job. If they have a decent job, then they can go into that factory and pay off the debt at the lower 'family' rate that the brick masters set.

As the plane landed back at Heathrow, my mind was set. We had to do something.

We picked up our bags from the carousel, went through customs and out to the car park to find our car.

Before we even got into the car, Matt had a phone call. It was from an old friend who had worked with us years ago in Nigeria.

'Matt, I believe God has told me you are about to start a new project. And by way of confirmation that this is from Him, I'm sending you £10,000 towards it.'

Wow. When God speaks – He speaks!

Within less than a year, every penny came through for the new home in Pakistan.

A lot of the initial costs were paid for by Belinda. Belinda was an American friend. On one of our visits she had said to Matt that we should let her know if and when we undertook a new project. Matt called her with regard to Pakistan and the money was sent.

Belinda had been a carer for an older couple. When the couple died, Belinda became the sole beneficiary from their estate. Little did Belinda know at the time, but the estate was vast. By God's grace and Belinda's generosity, a large amount of this money is now finding its way into life-changing projects.

I had the privilege of spending time with Belinda a few months before she herself died. Her giving to the mission field lives on as the best memorial anyone could ask for.

To date, we have fifty-two rescued kids from the brick factories. All now in education so that in the future they can gain real employment, pay off their families' debts and see the whole family set free from slavery once and for all.

These children can be children for the first time in their lives. Up until their rescue they'd only ever known how to be slaves. One of the most precious things we have seen is the children learning to play. They had never played a game in their lives before and are now rediscovering their childhood. The home is managed by a husband-and-wife team and it's right next to a school where just a year previously we had helped to build a playground.

Striking the Ground

While we were in Pakistan for the opening ceremony, we went back into the brick factories. This time felt even worse than the first time. On my first visit I was just in so much shock that I couldn't process what I was seeing. But this time I was well aware of the hopelessness in front of me.

I sat on a pile of bricks, playing pat-a-cake with a little girl who looked about four of five years of age. Before I knew it I was surrounded by all these little faces; young lives controlled by brick masters who wouldn't allow them to leave the factory. I was over the moon for the fifty-two now in our care, but what about the hundreds and thousands more that are still trapped in slavery? It felt like it broke me at that moment.

How do you stop it? How do you start to say 'enough is enough' to the brick masters? How do you strike the ground and declare enough in such a desperate and demoralising situation?

You know discouragement can stop you from striking the ground just as much as complacency or fear can. But strike the ground we must.

I'm referring to the scripture in 2 Kings 13 when Elisha is angry with the king for only striking the ground three times – the king's lack-lustre response showed the apathy in his heart. I desperately want to strike the ground in my life. And to keep striking. And keep striking.

We had struck the ground once with the Dignity Project. We had struck the ground again with this children's home. But there is more striking to be done in that land.

We suddenly had this ridiculous idea. If we can't get all the kids out of the factories, then could we get into the factories? What if, just for one hour a week, we could go into multiple brick factories with

Sunday school? What if, just for that hour, those beautiful children can be children again? What if, just for that hour, they can have fun, be loved, and most of all be introduced to Jesus? Will it fix the problem of them being in slavery? No. Not yet. But will it have an eternal consequence on their lives? Absolutely!

It seemed like madness. What slave master in his right mind would allow such a distraction in his factory every week? It had never been done before. It would be out of the question, right? But you never know until you strike the ground.

By the grace of God, several brick masters are now allowing us to set up Sunday Schools in their factories. As I write this there are Sunday Schools in 24 factories and we are reaching over 450 children trapped in slavery. We are still contending for their complete freedom but are thrilled that we can reach them with the love, hope and joy of Jesus.

I'm not sure I entirely know why the brick factory owners have allowed us in, I don't really understand their motives, but all I know is we're going to keep striking the ground in those factories as much as we can, because we don't know what tomorrow holds.

Whether it's thousands of kids in Kenya or hundreds of kids in Pakistan, our heart is the same; It's OneByOne. We continue to stop for the one. When we see the need, we stop and, with God's help, we strike the ground. I want to use my time well. I want to strike the ground in that nation like it's never been struck before, before it's too late.

Now new areas of Pakistan are beginning to open up. Matt managed to travel to the north of Pakistan, close to the Afghanistan border, to see if we're able to help girls who have fled from the Taliban. It's very sensitive work and not something we can write about here but, needless to say, we want to strike the ground again and again in Pakistan.

Growing

It's so good to see the ministry continue to grow. I'm grateful for every one of our volunteers, for every donation, big and small. God has blessed us with being able to present a regular programme on TBN Christian television – the title of this book comes from that programme. And more recently I've also started to broadcast on UCB Radio. We have featured on the BBC, Premier Radio, Revelation TV and the 700 Club.

Someone once said that Matt and I carry the heartbeat of God for the poor and needy. That's quite a compliment, but yes, that's how it feels sometimes. There are many others with us, and we plan to do all we can to fulfil that heartbeat of God. We plan to go where no one else will go. We plan to go – to continue to go – to the poorest of the poor. To stop for the one.

All from a girl with a chocolate bar watching the starving children of Africa. All from buying fifty-pence flip-flops for a girl in Sierra Leone. All from God encounters in a Pensacola car park, in a bamboo hut and witnessing a ship sail from a port.

Drinking from the Overflow

My lasting thankfulness for all we have done with OneByOne is to God, our provider. We've never had any millionaires bail us out, but He always brings in the finances at the moment we need it. He has never let us down. It's always enough. There is never any to spare, but there's never a lack.

He provided food from a blue container, supernaturally multiplying the food we needed. He put $50 into my hand on a day when I felt I was losing everything. He is a good God. He provides.

I want to finish this book with a story. A vision actually.

Back in 2007, Matt, working as a Christian journalist, had a commission to interview Ken Gott for a magazine. This was before we knew Ken and Lois so I decided to tag along as Matt's photographer.

All I had to do was to take some photos and stay quiet. I managed the first of these, but not quite the second.

The interview was in the House of Prayer in Sunderland, in one of the back offices. In the main room worship music was playing as background for the twenty-four-hour prayer that carried on there. Suddenly, part way through Matt's interview, something changed. I assumed that the CD that had been playing had been replaced by someone singing live. Suddenly, there was a real sense of God's presence.

I interrupted the interview.

'Do you guys feel that? Something's just shifted.'

'Yes,' said Ken, 'you're right. Let's go and see.'

And with that, the interview was over and Ken was on his way into the auditorium.

Matt gave me a glance that said something along the lines of 'you only had one job to do, to just stay quiet . . '.

It wasn't a live singer, just a different CD playing, by someone called Kim Clement. The worship was beautiful and the presence of God could almost be touched.

I found a corner just to lie in – to lie in God's presence and to soak in that presence.

Suddenly I was in a vision. In this vision, I was holding a cup with just a bit of red juice in it. As I held it, a little boy came along and, tugging at my trouser leg, he asked for a drink. I gave what was left to him and the cup was now empty.

The problem was that in my vision, hundreds of other children were now arriving, all of them asking for a drink, but I had nothing left. I began to panic.

In the vision, I turned and held the cup up towards heaven. Then I saw a golden flow of water from heaven. It filled the cup. But what was interesting was that the children around me didn't drink directly from the cup or ask for a drink from the cup. Instead they ran under the golden overflow from my cup.

Instantly I knew what the Holy Spirit was telling me. There's no point giving a thirsty world a drink from an empty cup.

Sometimes we can be performing the right actions, bending down and sharing our cup with others, but if our cups are empty the whole thing is meaningless. How many times have we tried to help thirsty, needy people and we wonder why they're still in a mess? If our cup is empty there's only one thing for us to do. We must stop. We must seek a new source.

Too often we look at the need. But if we just keep our eyes fixed on Him, He will provide. My empty cup will not do the job. The golden overflow of water will.

Maybe today is about you lifting up your cup, lifting up your life, lifting up your empty vessel to heaven; fixing your eyes back on your first love.

The vision has stayed with me. It was long before we had our first children's home. My dreams were still dreams. My calling was not yet fully formed.

But at that moment I knew that whatever I faced, whatever the challenges, I was always going to lift the cup to heaven.

And over the years, by God's grace, I have seen the overflow.

I don't have everything figured out. I don't have a twenty-year plan for global domination with OneByOne. But I look to Him. I lift my cup to Him.

And I trust. I continue to trust. I trust Him for His provision.

Invitation

Thank you for reading my story. Life is a gift from God. It's an opportunity to experience, first hand, the most thrilling love story ever told. Walking with Jesus is more fulfilling than anything this world could ever offer. Let him lead you on the greatest adventure, as you too, begin to Embrace the Journey.

Becky

For more information on any of our work please visit:
www.onebyone.net or you can email us at **admin@onebyone.net**

About the Authors

Becky Murray is the founder and director of OneByOne. She serves as a missionary around the world. Becky can be seen on her programme *Embrace the Journey* on TBN and has her own programme on UCB Radio. Becky is married to Matt and they serve as senior pastors at Renew Church, Uttoxeter.

Ralph Turner is the author of a number of books, including *Greater Things,* the story of the New Wine movement, and his well-received biography *Gerald Coates – Pioneer.* Ralph is married to Roh and they are part of Chroma Church, Leicester.